"*Transformational Frontiers* is a needed reminder that development work falls short if it does not integrate the development of the whole person: spirit, soul, and body. Therefore, the body of Christ is uniquely positioned to carry out true development work. While this book focuses on professional development workers and agencies (NGOs), the same principles apply to every follower of Christ and every church worldwide. If the entire body of Christ would recognize its responsibilities in this arena, that would dwarf all the work and impact from NGOs and professional development workers."

—Curtis Sergeant

Author of *The Only One: Living Fully In, By, and For God*

"At a time when the role of international NGOs is undergoing increasing scrutiny regarding their impact, Dr. Jaisankar Sarma's book, *Transformational Frontiers*, is an important contribution to this discussion. He highlights a handful of issues that need to be addressed in order to improve effectiveness. Jaisankar is right when he says that our vision needs to be on nurturing local processes of growth, renewal, and kingdom witness and not on organizational survival."

—Rupen Das

Research Professor, Tyndale University

"This is a remarkable and long-overdue work. Drawing on research and over forty years of experience, from community work in India to global leadership with World Vision International, Jai reveals how a focus on short-term deliverables undermines the adaptive journey to transformational change with vulnerable communities. With honesty and compassion, he examines the system end to end, highlighting frontline pressures. His prophetic insights have already influenced World Vision and called us back to our mission."

—Camilla Symes

Global Director of Transformational Development, World Vision International

"In *Transformational Frontiers*, Jai Sarma, makes it clear: if our poverty alleviation initiatives are to be transformational in the way Jesus intends, we must take seriously the formation, agency, and voice of the grassroots development practitioners. Sarma draws on decades of experience to prove his point and offers indispensable insights into how it's done. His message is vital not only for Christian development executives, but donor agencies, church partners, scholars, and theologians—anyone who has influence on Christian relief and development initiatives."

—Tim Swauger

President, South Asia Access

"This book should be essential reading for all leadership teams of Christian NGOs—Jaisankar offers deep insight and challenge on how organizations can support fieldworkers, empowering them for great kingdom impact rather than unintentionally constraining, frustrating, and limiting their contribution. Even before finishing the book, I began reflecting on practical ways we could better support the 'hands and feet' of our work—the people whose presence and voices embody our mission on the ground."

—Myles Harrison

Chief Operating Officer, Edify

"Christian development ministry has often lacked full awareness of fieldworkers' agency in delivering impact. Jaisankar brilliantly bridges this gap through highlighting their essential role as actors with agency and as witnesses to Christ in communities they serve. This is not the work of an armchair specialist; it arises from Jaisankar's passion for transformational development and his own presence in communities and the fieldworkers whom he places on the pedestal they deserve. It is as much a critique of the impersonal systems as of the institutions that create them. His argument is not that quantifiable productivity is insignificant but rather that this does not have priority over the real stories of fieldworkers' incarnational presence in communities."

—David Emmanuel Singh

Institutional Link Tutor, Middlesex University

Transformational Frontiers

Transformational Frontiers

Bridging Communities and Christian NGOs in Practice

JAISANKAR SARMA

Foreword by Alexia Salvatierra

☙PICKWICK *Publications* · Eugene, Oregon

TRANSFORMATIONAL FRONTIERS
Bridging Communities and Christian NGOs in Practice

Copyright © 2025 Jaisankar Sarma. All rights reserved. Except for brief quotations in critical publications or reviews, no part of this book may be reproduced in any manner without prior written permission from the publisher. Write: Permissions, Wipf and Stock Publishers, 199 W. 8th Ave., Suite 3, Eugene, OR 97401.

Pickwick Publications
An Imprint of Wipf and Stock Publishers
199 W. 8th Ave., Suite 3
Eugene, OR 97401

www.wipfandstock.com

PAPERBACK ISBN: 979-8-3852-0966-8
HARDCOVER ISBN: 979-8-3852-0967-5
EBOOK ISBN: 979-8-3852-0968-2

Cataloguing-in-Publication data:

Names: Jaisankar, Sarma, author. | Salvatierra, Alexia, 1956–, foreword.

Title: Transformational frontiers : bridging communities and Christian NGOs in practice / Sarma Jaisankar ; foreword by Alexia Salvatierra.

Description: Eugene, OR : Pickwick Publications, 2025 | Includes bibliographical references and index.

Identifiers: ISBN 979-8-3852-0966-8 (paperback) | ISBN 979-8-3852-0967-5 (hardcover) | ISBN 979-8-3852-0968-2 (ebook)

Subjects: LCSH: Missions. | Non-governmental organizations. | Communities—Religious aspects—Christianity. | Holism.

Classification: BV2061.3 J35 2025 (paperback) | BV2061.3 (ebook)

VERSION NUMBER 121625

Scriptures are from THE HOLY BIBLE, NEW INTERNATIONAL VERSION®, NIV® Copyright © 1973, 1978, 1984, 2011 by Biblica, Inc.® Used by permission. All rights reserved worldwide.

Dedication

To my Lord and Savior, Jesus Christ,
The Perfect Fieldworker,
You left the splendor of your home,
Came to us incarnate in flesh,
Walked the dusty roads,
Touched the lepers,
Healed the broken-hearted,
Washed our feet,
And paid the ultimate price.

In your life, you showed us how to live.
In your death, you redeemed us.
In your resurrection, you gave us life.
In your ascension, you empowered us through your Holy Spirit.
You formed us into a new community.

May we follow you and your example
In serving the least of our brothers and sisters
Whom you have called us to love.
May your kingdom and your glory be our heartbeat.
May you accept this book as a humble offering in this pursuit.

Contents

List of Diagrams and Tables | ix
Foreword by Alexia Salvatierra | xi
Preface | xiii
Acknowledgments | xxi
List of Abbreviations | xxiii

Introduction: Essence of Transformational Development | 1
1 At the Heart of Transformation: The Role of Fieldworkers | 19
2 Theories of Development and the Role of Fieldworkers: Why Theories Matter | 46
3 Between Metrics and Mission: Organizational Strategy and Field Practice—The Call to Spirit-Led Strategy | 73
4 Evangelism and Church Partnerships Within the Context of Holistic Ministry: The Place of Evangelism in Holistic Ministry | 103
5 Framing the Fieldworker's Role in Organizational Life | 134
6 Catalysts of Kingdom Movements: When the Mission Is Complete | 153

Bibliography | 173
Index | 179

Diagrams and Tables

Diagram 1.1—Fieldworker Tension | 38

Table 2.1—Fieldworker Roles Across Development Paradigms: A Comparative Overview | 49

Diagram 2.1—Weaving Development | 68

Diagram 3.1—Strategy to Programming Cascade | 81

Diagram 3.2—Ideal Scenario of Fieldworker Mediating Strategy and M&E | 100

Diagram 4.1—An Adapted Version of Harden's Typology of Integration Models | 107

Table 6.1—Fieldworker's Role in TD Process | 158

Diagram 6.1—Disciple Multiplication | 162

Foreword

I HAVE STARTED AND managed eight nonprofit faith-based organizations in my life, of different sizes and in various countries. In each context, we have consistently struggled with the tension between adhering to our mission and raising funds. Sustaining the work financially requires proving its value to those who give or allocate funds, typically through meeting metrics that are easily measured. The deeper, more complex goals of transforming lives and relationships and the sensitivity to the movement of the Spirit required to achieve those goals are not so easily measured.

Reading *Transformational Frontiers*, with its eloquent portrayals of heroic fieldworkers in the development arena struggling with systems that do not completely support their work, echoes and illuminates these parallel and painful tensions. With exquisite precision, Jaisankar Sarma lays out the components of transformational development work on the ground in some of the most unpredictable and resource-poor contexts in the world. Drawing from a lifetime of experience as well as a broad theoretical landscape, he describes the necessary conditions for faithful and effective holistic mission as well as the theories of change, structures, and policies that create (or fail to create) those conditions.

The variety of specific prescriptions described for different areas of transformational development work in the field is impressive. Dr. Sarma offers advice on how to recruit, train, mentor, and spiritually sustain fieldworkers. He unsparingly demonstrates the impact of rigid, top-down planning and bureaucratic record-keeping on the work on the ground, quenching the Spirit and the creative potential for adaptive leadership. He also shines a light on the relationship between fundraising and the captivity of fieldworkers to narrow, secular metrics that do not allow time and space for organic processes of empowerment and substantive change.

Thankfully, the book goes beyond criticism to cast an alternative vision of collaboration between field and management, in which quantitative and qualitative evaluation are appropriately integrated and technical expertise is placed at the service of incarnational accompaniment. Dr. Sarma also recognizes that another level of collaboration is necessary beyond fieldworkers and management in order to carry out God's plan for transformational development; he spends a chapter discussing the problems and possibilities for integrating evangelism and church partnership into the development process. His suggestion to tie transformational development more closely to the disciple making and church planting movements feels prophetic; God is already at work seeding this beautiful possibility.

Perhaps the most powerful characteristic of this book is its array of stories. The principles that Jaisankar Sarma offers are enfleshed in moving and touching stories that are impossible to disregard.

With all of its useful detail and beautiful stories, the challenge at the heart of the book is both simple and profound. What does our work to improve the lives and communities of the poor and marginalized look like if we really recognize that God is the agent of development? What courageous risks would we take? How might we structure our work to prioritize faithfulness to mission over guaranteeing funding? How would we make sure that we don't gain the world and lose our souls? While Jaisankar Sarma is exploring the answer to those questions in the development arena, his work is provocative for any of us who are struggling with similar tensions in our ministries.

I am a Lutheran pastor; I have been formed as a disciple to live with a two kingdoms orientation. We know that we live in the in-between time between the first and second coming of Christ. We recognize that in this time, we live on this side of the cross, where we must struggle with the realities of human carnal limitations as well as the negative power of individual and corporate sinfulness. Yet, we also know that there are moments when the kingdom of God breaks in, giving us a foretaste of the feast to come. If we are too focused on the reality of the kingdom of this world, we will miss the opportunity to experience the kingdom of God in our midst. This book opens our eyes to the presence and power of that kingdom and calls us to make space for its fullest expression in the development field—and beyond.

Dr. Alexia Salvatierra,
Academic Dean for Centro Latino
and Associate Professor of Mission and Global Transformation,
Fuller Theological Seminary

Preface

WHY I WROTE THIS BOOK

I HAVE HAD THE privilege of working in the field of transformational development for nearly four decades. From my early days as a technical worker in the field to my later role as the vice president of World Vision International, I have walked alongside people and programs in diverse cultural and organizational settings. From remote villages to boardrooms, my experiences have shown me that the heart of transformation does not reside in strategy documents, program models, or evaluation frameworks. Rather, the heart of transformational development lives and breathes in the daily, faithful work of fieldworkers—those who walk dusty roads, sit in homes and under trees, and immerse themselves in the everyday realities of people and communities.

Time and again, I have seen that it is fieldworkers who are central to facilitating holistic change in people's lives. They are not merely implementers of plans, nor are they passive instruments of external interventions. Fieldworkers bear Christ's love, mediate trust, facilitate local vision, and witness to the gospel through word and deed. Yet, despite their central role, Christian development agencies increasingly prioritize strategies, program models, metrics, and managerial efficiency—everything but the fieldworkers and their capacity to act. I have met inspired, empowered fieldworkers who are catalysts of transformation. But I have also encountered deeply frustrated fieldworkers, who are constrained by systems, boxed in by rigid protocols, and who feel more like instruments than agents. This book is a tribute to them. You will meet some of them in the chapters ahead.

My primary purpose in writing this book is to lift up the critical role that fieldworkers play in Christ-centered development. At its core,

Preface

Transformational Development is about God's mission in the world. We are not the initiators or owners of transformation: God is. But God invites us, especially those on the front lines, to become co-laborers in the renewal of all things. I have also observed a troubling trend in the practice of holistic ministry. The desire to be "holistic" has sometimes become an excuse to dilute the witness of Christ. While I affirm the need to address physical, social, and emotional needs, it is problematic when the spiritual dimension, our intentional witness to the gospel of Jesus Christ, is sidelined or assumed. Christian organizations involved in development work have come to rely too heavily on good deeds and hope that these will somehow speak for themselves. Evangelism without mercy and justice is not holistic. Similarly, mercy and justice without a clear witness to the good news of Jesus Christ is not holistic, either. Christ's call is to be both salt and light.

The relational element between fieldworkers and community members, so strongly emphasized in the literature of the seventies and eighties, no longer seems to hold the same priority. Relationships have been pushed to the margins, while strategies, best practices, and performance metrics have taken center stage. In the pursuit of professionalism, efficiency, scalability, and funding, development has been depersonalized. Christian organizations have reduced transformational development to time-bound, project-driven efforts, rather than Spirit-empowered movements rooted in incarnational presence and authentic relationships. This book aims to re-center relationships as core to transformational development.

INTENDED AUDIENCE

This book is written first and foremost for those who have the power to shape the practice of transformational development: Christian NGO leaders, program managers, field coordinators, and the fieldworkers themselves. Churches that are involved in holistic community development might also find this work useful. I hope that this work can be a mirror, a conversation partner, and perhaps even a gentle challenge to see and better support grassroots efforts. I also hope students and scholars engaged in development studies, especially those exploring the intersection of faith and development, will find this book useful.

Preface

WHAT SHAPES MY VIEWS IN THIS BOOK

My journey into this work is deeply shaped by my personal faith and life experience. I came to know Christ as a young college student in India, having been raised in a different religious tradition. As I began to study the Scriptures, I came to understand that serving the poor was not simply a matter of compassion or charity: it was a direct expression of obedience to the Lordship of Christ. This conviction has profoundly influenced my life and career choices. Over the years, I have had the privilege of serving in a variety of contexts: first in India and later in Cambodia among subsistence farmers, before expanding into leadership roles across the Asia Pacific region and at a global level. I worship in churches that take their mission seriously by proclaiming Christ and serving the poor in their own local contexts. My doctoral research at the Oxford Centre for Mission Studies (UK) focused on fieldworkers and the tensions they navigate as they serve at the intersection of organizational expectations and the lived realities of the poor. Much of my career has been spent within World Vision, a large international Christian organization engaged in a broad scope of work. In more recent years, I have served with smaller, more focused Christian ministries. I have learned valuable lessons from both large and small organizations. Being small in size does not reduce importance; smaller ministries often demonstrate a depth of impact and agility that is equally vital to the work of transformational development. I have visited and worked in more than eighty countries, and I learned much from the diversity of cultures, expressions of faith, and local practices of ministry. These experiences, along with my education and theological formation, have undoubtedly shaped the way I see the world, how I understand transformational development, and how I write this book.

THE DEVELOPMENT LENS GUIDING THIS BOOK

This book is written from the perspective of a particular paradigm of development—Transformational Development (TD)—which refers to God's holistic, redemptive work. Though this book centers on local expressions, transformational development is fundamentally part of God's expansive mission to renew and restore all things—locally, globally, and cosmically. When such an understanding of Transformational Development shapes NGO-led project interventions, community-level engagement becomes grounded in a holistic approach that values the agency of local people. The focus on community-led initiatives does not negate the vital role of other development approaches that prioritize large-scale investments in infrastructure, health, education, agriculture, or policy reform. Such broader, system-level interventions are essential, especially in contexts of extreme poverty where, despite strong local leadership and initiative, the resources available through Christian organizations alone are insufficient to address the magnitude of need. Locally led transformational development rightly seeks to empower communities to build on their God-given assets and capabilities. At the same time, the structural barriers posed by systemic poverty, weak institutions, and political instability often require interventions that extend beyond the local level. In such contexts, community-driven efforts and externally supported programs must work hand-in-hand, with each respecting and reinforcing the other. Christian organizations are called to strengthen community agency and dignity while engaging wisely with broader systems to ensure that external assistance empowers rather than displaces local leadership. The scope of this book, however, remains centered on the practice of transformational development by Christian organizations working in partnership with local communities.

EMBEDDING MISSION: FIELDWORKERS WITHIN ORGANIZATIONAL SYSTEMS

This book does not intend to portray fieldworkers as the sole heroes of transformational development; they do not work in isolation. Rather, they serve within teams, under organizational systems, and alongside communities. Their work is woven into a larger tapestry of vision, mission, and collaboration. Yet within this framework, something essential is often overlooked: how fieldworkers bring their unique sense of calling, passion, and discernment into organizational contexts. They are not simply implementers. As agents of transformation, they are the hands and feet of the organization. Strategies and program models provide boundaries and tools, but the fieldworker's lived presence and Spirit-led wisdom can transform life. The question is not whether systems or individuals matter more but how the two can align. Organizational structures must make room for and be shaped by the calling and agency of those on the front lines.

Preface

The following vignettes are drawn from field interviews conducted in India in 2018. Each story reflects a different way in which fieldworkers, while operating within the same organization and program framework, express their work in deeply personal and contextually grounded ways. Their approaches varied, but each story serves the broader vision of transformation. Each fieldworker exercised judgment within the limits of organizational structure, and in doing so, they revealed the importance of aligning organizational mission with lived experience.

In one rural program, Rekha (not her real name[1]) served as a community development facilitator with a passion for healing broken relationships. Her work focused on community engagement and social transformation, but it was never only about activities or outputs. She often said, "My job is to promote transformation." What is transformation? For Rekha, it meant a change in how people related to one another and how they saw the world. In one village, caste divisions had split the community. People refused to draw water from the same well. Rekha initiated a peace committee that drew on Scripture and prayer and facilitated multiple meetings over time. Slowly, through respectful dialogue and persistent prayer, people agreed to use the same water source. In another community, Rekha worked with adolescent girls who were not allowed to ride bicycles or two-wheelers. Men would mock her when she rode her motorcycle. But she persisted. She taught girls how to cycle. Over time, attitudes shifted. It was not a quick change. It took time, conversation, and presence. Men who once scorned her began to see things differently. As she recounted these stories, Rekha highlighted that transformation must begin in people's thinking and in relationships. She emphasized that although child marriage, child labor, and open defecation may be visible development issues in her communities, change occurs by first confronting the beliefs and behaviors that sustain these practices. Programs can provide a platform, and budgets can fund programs, but lasting change requires being with people, listening, and walking patiently with them.

Another fieldworker, Arun, had a very different calling. For him, child protection was the heart of his work. Having lost his own young daughter, Arun brought a personal passion to issues of justice for children, particularly those children who had been abused. In the villages he served, he helped organize after-school tutoring programs, and he trained volunteers to monitor child rights violations. In one case, a powerful

---

1. I have changed the names of fieldworkers in case studies throughout the book.

man was abusing several children. The case was sensitive. Arun knew his organization preferred to avoid high-profile legal confrontations, and so he acted discreetly. He spent a week coordinating behind the scenes with the child protection unit, police, social welfare department, and local governance bodies. Arun informed his manager (in general terms), but he withheld names and details. The man was eventually arrested and sentenced to eighteen years in prison—with no mention of the organization in the media reports or police records. Arun's actions were deliberate, rooted in discernment, and guided by his deep sense of responsibility before God and his organization's guidelines and preferences. He often quoted Matt 25: "whatever you did for one of the least of these brothers and sisters of mine, you did it for me." During our interview, he reflected on the importance of listening to children and of being sensitive to their needs. Arun's work was deeply impactful. Helping even a few children through school can have a ripple effect on families and communities.

A third fieldworker, Sanjay, approached his role through the lens of systems and connections. He was known for his meticulous documentation and wide-ranging networks. Sanjay kept journals of every child with a disability in his area, along with photos, case notes, and follow-up actions. He had a detailed register of resources he had mobilized from outside partners over the years, including funds, materials, and technical support. These resources did not pass through organizational accounts, but they all reached the community. In one month alone, Sanjay mobilized nearly three hundred thousand rupees to establish a tailoring unit for women to learn the skill and earn an income. He made sure that co-branded events acknowledged partner contributions, and he often invited the local press to cover collaborative efforts. Sanjay's belief was simple: development did not depend solely on his organization's money. There were abundant resources in government and civil society, but most assets were not reaching the communities. His task was to build those bridges. Sanjay insisted that partnerships be mutually beneficial. He sought equity and transparency in all collaborations. Because of his reliability and posture of service, many partner agencies preferred to work through him, even when he introduced them to his fellow fieldworkers.

What stands out in these three stories is not just the variety of approaches, but these fieldworkers' freedom, creativity, and courage. Their work was not prescribed in detail by program plans. Rather, it emerged from conviction, context, and calling. All three operated under the same program goal: protecting children from violence. Each contributed to that goal in unique ways that were shaped by their own life, experience, and understanding of mission. Their decisions often fell outside official budgets and plans, and yet they moved the work forward in profound ways. Transformational development happens when organizations allow space for such agency and when structures support the Spirit's work through ordinary people. Fieldworkers like Rekha, Arun, and Sanjay show that it is possible to be faithful both to organizational vision and personal calling. When this alignment happens, transformation becomes not only a goal but a way of life. In this book, we will explore how the agency of fieldworkers and supportive organizational structures can work together to amplify the Spirit's work through local leaders, promoting transformational development.

This book invites readers to see transformational development not primarily through the lens of organizational strategies or systems but through the lives of those who walk day-by-day alongside people within their communities. This book calls for a recovery of the centrality of fieldworkers and a reimagined organizational practice that honors their calling, agency, and witness to Christ.

Acknowledgments

I AM DEEPLY THANKFUL to God for the incredible gift of learning from so many fieldworkers over the years. I have had the privilege of sitting with them, listening to their stories—what inspired them, what kept them going, what made them proud, and what left them frustrated. I have prayed with them, laughed and celebrated with them, and also listened to their pains and struggles. There are far too many to name, but their faith, humility, courage, and perseverance have shaped me more than any textbook or theory ever could. Many of their stories—and the stories they shared with me—are woven throughout this book.

I am also deeply thankful to World Vision, an organization with which I have been long associated. It was through my years of service with World Vision that I truly learned the practice of development. If anything in this book reads as a critique of World Vision or its practices, it is also, in a very real sense, a critique of myself. I was part of shaping many of those policies and decisions, and I write with humility—and with hope—that we can continue to grow and do better. I am grateful to many colleagues in World Vision whose friendship, insights, and collaboration over the years have deeply enriched me. Much of what I have written reflects what I have learned from them. I would like especially to acknowledge Bryant Myers, who has served as both mentor and supervisor to me over many years. His perspective on holism and development has profoundly shaped my thinking, and as you will see throughout this book, I have drawn extensively from his writings.

I am grateful to Heaven's Family for introducing me to the powerful opportunity of integrating holistic community development with Disciple Making Movements (DMM), and to Curtis Sergeant for training me—and countless others—in the principles and practices of DMM. I have witnessed this integration in a few contexts, and its impact for advancing God's kingdom is both significant and deeply encouraging.

I also want to thank Dr. Katy Attanasi for her invaluable editorial assistance. Her careful reading, insightful suggestions, and generous support helped improve the clarity and coherence of this manuscript.

I want to express my deepest gratitude to my wife, Saro, and our two children, Joshua and Pavithra, whose quiet strength and unwavering love have sustained me through these many years of work. They have given me the freedom to pursue this calling—often at great personal cost. Their patience, prayers, and faithful presence have been a steady source of encouragement and grace. I could not have undertaken this journey without them.

Abbreviations

CCT	Church and Community Transformation
CMA	Christian Missionary Alliance
CPM	Church Planting Movements
CVA	Citizen Voice and Action
DMM	Disciple Making Movements
ECD	Early Childhood Development
FGW	Farming God's Way
GLG	God's Love Group
HDI	Human Development Index
ICM	International Care Ministries
INGO	International Non-Governmental Organization
KPI	Key Performance Indicators
M&E	Monitoring and Evaluation
NGO	Non-Governmental Organization
OMF	Overseas Missionary Fellowship
PLA	Participatory Learning and Action
RAA	Richarry-Ayllu Association
SDG	Sustainable Development Goal
SIM	Sudan Interior Mission
SWOT	Strengths, Weaknesses, Opportunities, and Threats
TD	Transformational Development
TDI	Transformational Development Indicators
TEAM	The Evangelical Alliance Mission
USAID	United States Agency for International Development

Introduction
Essence of Transformational Development

It seems only fitting to begin this book by articulating my core understanding of Transformational Development (TD)—not because others have not said it better, but because any meaningful exploration of this topic must begin with clarity about the biblical convictions that shape its content. Christian non-governmental organizations (NGOs) such as Food for the Hungry, World Vision, and others, along with academic institutions like Fuller Theological Seminary, the Oxford Centre for Mission Studies, and Asian Theological Seminary, commonly use the term *Transformational Development* to describe their approach. In contrast, organizations like Tearfund, Micah Global, and others prefer the term *Integral Mission*. While the terminology varies, both expressions reflect a shared commitment to placing the Christian faith at the center of development practice—emphasizing the integration of spiritual, social, and material transformation.[1]

For Christian organizations engaged in TD, development is not merely a technical task to advance human progress or advocacy work to change the systems and structure. As part of the church's broader participation in God's mission in the world, the work of justice, healing, and restoration are ways to respond faithfully to the call of Christ. As David Bosch reminds us, this understanding places TD firmly within the larger biblical vision of mission. The quote that follows captures the impetus for transformational development as part of God's redemptive purposes for the world through the church:

---

1. Gorlorwulu and Rachschulte, "Organizational and Leadership Implications."

> The missionary task is the whole church bringing the whole gospel to the whole world. People live in a series of integrated relationships; it is therefore indicative of a false anthropology and sociology to divorce the spiritual or the personal sphere from the material and the social. God's love and attention are directed primarily at the world, and mission is "participation in God's existence in the world." In our time, God's yes to the world reveals itself, to a large extent, in the church's missionary engagement in respect of the realities of injustice, oppression, poverty, discrimination, and violence.[2]

This faith-rooted understanding of TD undergirds everything I have written in this book.

A NOTE ON TERMINOLOGY

I would like to clarify briefly some terminology used throughout this book, especially given the nuanced ways in which terms like Transformational Development, Holistic Ministry, and Integral Mission are applied in different ministry and organizational contexts.

I use the terms *Transformational Development*, *Holistic Ministry*, and *Integral Mission* interchangeably, while acknowledging their distinct origins and emphases. *Transformational Development* serves as my primary framing term; it refers to an integrated vision of change that brings the measurable improvements in people's material and social conditions together with the deeper, internal transformations in values, identity, and worldview. This vision is rooted in an understanding of the kingdom of God as both present and yet to come, which calls people to pursue justice, peace, and restored relationships in all areas of life.[3] *Integral Mission*, a term more commonly used in the Latin American context, emphasizes the inseparability of gospel proclamation and social action, and it challenges false dichotomies between evangelism and development.[4] A third term, *Holistic Ministry*, describes the practical outworking of this integrated vision: reaching a community with the whole gospel for the whole person through whole churches that integrate evangelism and social action to

---

2. Bosch, *Transforming Mission*, 10.
3. Myers, *Walking with the Poor*, 177–283.
4. Yamamori and Padilla, *Local Church*, 22–35.

address both spiritual and physical needs.[5] Though each term carries its own theological and regional nuance, they all point toward a unified commitment to witness, service, and transformation in the name of Christ. One more point of clarification: Christian organization-led interventions may be referred to as transformational development (lowercase) when they align with the broader vision of what God is doing. Such efforts humbly acknowledge their place within God's larger mission of renewal and restoration.

In this book, I use the terms *Christian organizations* and *Christian NGOs* broadly to refer to local, national, and international entities, including churches, faith-based nonprofits, and mission agencies that engage in service and ministry among the poor. While these organizations may differ in structure, scale, and theological tradition, they share a common commitment to expressing the love of Christ through practical action. Whether formally registered as NGOs or operating informally through local churches and grassroots initiatives, these organizations play a vital role in responding to human need, promoting justice, and bearing witness to the gospel in word and deed.

MY PERSPECTIVES ON TRANSFORMATIONAL DEVELOPMENT

Having outlined the key terms, I now turn to the core principles I consider essential for authentic Transformational Development. This list is not exhaustive, but it seeks to highlight convictions that, in my view, are central to a biblically grounded and contextually engaged practice. I have framed these principles primarily as reflections of the broader redemptive work that God is accomplishing in the world—calling individuals, communities, and systems toward justice, reconciliation, and holistic flourishing—though they may carry some organizational implications as well.

1. God is the main agent of Transformational Development

At the heart of Transformational Development (TD) lies the conviction that ultimately God brings about transformation, which implies a redemptive, inside-out change, and affects not just external conditions but the beliefs,

---

5. Sider et al., "Holistic Ministry Defined."

attitudes, behaviors, and actions of individuals and communities. Such change cannot be orchestrated merely by human effort; it is God's Spirit working in the lives of people and within systems. The phrase *transformational development* brings together two important concepts—*transformation* and *development*—each carrying distinct but complementary meanings. The *Cambridge Dictionary* defines transformation as "a complete change in the appearance or character of something or someone, especially so that that thing or person is improved,"[6] while the *Oxford Dictionary* adds that it involves "a change in form, shape, appearance—metamorphosis."[7] The term *metamorphosis* evokes the image of a caterpillar becoming a butterfly, which symbolizes the kind of profound, inner change that TD seeks to embody. In contrast, the word *development*, defined by *Oxford Dictionary* as "a process of growth or change, often towards a more advanced or improved state,"[8] typically refers to incremental, observable, and often measurable change, usually in material or structural terms.

When these two terms are brought together as *transformational development*, the phrase conveys a holistic process in which deep, internal change, rooted in personal and communal transformation, lays the foundation for sustainable, measurable, and outward progress. This understanding of TD sees development not only as external progress but as a reflection of the inner work of God in people and systems. It affirms that the spiritual and the material are not separate realms but are part of God's mission to restore all things. The arena of this transformation is the world itself, which God is reconciling to himself through Christ. As Paul writes in Colossians, "through him [God] reconciled to himself all things, whether things on earth or things in heaven" (1:19–20 NIV). Until that reconciliation is complete, we are invited to participate in God's mission, through the many expressions of ministry and service entrusted to the church.

2. The goal of TD is both inner transformation and improved well-being

The connection between inner transformation and outward development lies at the heart of the twofold goal of Transformational Development. As

6. Cambridge Dictionary, s.v. "transformation."
7. Oxford English Dictionary, s.v. "transformation."
8. Oxford English Dictionary, s.v. "development."

Bryant Myers describes, TD seeks both: (a) Changed People: those who have rediscovered their identity as children of God and reclaimed their vocation as stewards of God's creation; and (b) Changed Relationships: relationships that are just, peaceful, and life-giving across all dimensions of life.[9] The Bible expresses this vision through rich theological images: *abundant life*, *shalom*, *new creation*, and the *restoration of broken relationships*, whether within individuals and families, among communities and nations, or in relationship to creation itself. At the heart of it all is the conviction that God is making all things new (Rev 21:5), and Transformational Development is one expression of our participation in that redemptive work. The goal of TD, therefore, is not simply to help the poor attain the lifestyles of those in high- or middle-income contexts. Rather, it reflects a fundamentally different understanding of human flourishing. Secular development theory, particularly in its Enlightenment and positivist forms, often assumes that human progress is linear, controllable, and measurable, and achieved through rational planning and empirical methods without reference to spiritual or relational dimensions.[10] Within that framework, development is driven by external intervention, expertise, and the logic of technical solutions. By contrast, Transformational Development affirms that true human flourishing cannot be reduced to material indicators alone. While access to resources, services, and opportunities is essential, particularly for those who are poor or vulnerable, TD insists that development be grounded in restored identity, relationships, and purpose. It draws on the biblical vision of *eternal life* and *abundant life*, not only in the future, but as a present reality rooted in justice, peace, dignity, and hope. The goal is not merely improvement but also transformation, people and communities who become fully alive, in right relationship with God, with one another, and with creation.

3. We are co-laborers with God in TD

God is continually at work among people to bring about Transformational Development. God in his grace invites us to be co-laborers in that work, not as saviors of the poor but as companions on their journey toward wholeness and restoration. Each person, including those who are poor and vulnerable, is created in the image of a creative and redemptive God. Our calling is

---

9. Myers, *Walking with the Poor*, 190–202.
10. Cowen and Shenton, *Doctrines of Development*, 27.

not to rescue but to walk alongside and to bear witness to God's presence and purposes already at work in their lives. Our engagement begins with the offering of our lives to God. As Rom 12:1 reminds us, transformation begins when we present ourselves as living sacrifices, yielded and responsive to God's will. In this process, we are both disciples and disciple makers, and we recognize that only a transformed life can help nurture transformation in others. We do not separate our life from our work; both are part of the same calling. Our contributions, whether brief or enduring, large or small, are always finite and imperfect. Yet we trust that God weaves them into a much larger story. Others have gone before us, and others will follow after us to build upon the foundation we help to lay. Our role is to stay attuned to what God is already doing in the lives of people and communities, and to align our work with his redemptive movement. To do this well, we rely on God's guidance. We give space for worship, prayer, fasting, and reflection on scripture as essential and regular parts of our work and not as occasional extras. These spiritual disciplines sustain our vision and posture of dependence, and when we see fruit and transformation taking root, we give glory to God. Neither our cleverness nor our effort brings about true change; it is the power of God working in and through us.

4. We approach TD work in humility

We enter with humility the life worlds of people who are poor and adopt a position of listening and learning. We recognize that God is already present and at work among them, and we honor the unique gifts, insights, and dignity they carry. We take time to understand their history, context, needs, opportunities, and struggles, and we seek to see through their eyes and hear with their voices. This practice of understanding requires setting aside our own assumptions, biases, and professional expertise in order to engage with respect and openness. We do not impose our own agendas. Rather, we support communities as they analyze their own challenges and take initiative in addressing them by drawing on their own knowledge, relationships, and resources. Where appropriate, we bring our expertise and resources to complement but never to replace their efforts. We offer what we have both to God and the communities we serve: our skills, experiences, networks, finances, and most importantly, our faith and trust in God. Ultimately, we expect God to do far more than we could ever accomplish on our own. The transformation we seek is not the sum of our inputs but the fruit of God's grace and power working in and through people, including ourselves, in ways far beyond what we could plan or predict.

5. TD work is always holistic

Transformational Development is, by its very nature, holistic. While each of us may be called to specific and focused work, our understanding of TD remains comprehensive and encompasses individuals, families, communities, nations, and ultimately, the whole of creation. A holistic approach means we see people not in isolation but as whole persons living within a web of relationships and systems—social, economic, political, cultural, and spiritual. Even when our work is concentrated in a particular area, we intentionally seek holistic impact and recognize that life is interconnected and cannot be compartmentalized. TD reflects an integrated view of humanity, body and soul, spirit and matter, and it refuses to treat people as fragmented beings. Though we long and pray for the people we serve to enter God's kingdom, we do not use development work as a platform to impose our Christian faith on others. We do not pit development against evangelism nor debate their relative importance. We see them as inseparable. We demonstrate the gospel through lives marked by love and service, and when appropriate, we also share the good news in word—always with humility, gentleness, and respect. We do not divide life into sacred and secular compartments; we affirm that God is active in all areas of human life, and that all our work, when done in Christ's name, is spiritual.

6. By its very nature, TD is mutual in its effects

Transformational Development is inherently mutual and never one-directional. No one can engage in TD without being changed in the process. Transformation impacts everyone: the poor and the non-poor, donors and recipients, fieldworkers, staff, service providers, and clients. As Myers reminds us, transformation for the poor comes as they rediscover their identity as children of God, reclaim their God-given vocation, and enter into restored relationships—relationships that support and empower rather than diminish them. The non-poor, too, are transformed as they relinquish their god-complexes and come to see their wealth and resources not as personal entitlements but as gifts meant to be shared.[11] In this mutual journey, fieldworkers and staff often find their own values, lifestyles, and spiritual commitments reshaped by their relationships with the poor. They learn from the generosity, resilience, and faith of those they serve. At the same time, the poor are not expected to emulate the lifestyles of the powerful or affluent but to remain rooted in their dignity as image-bearers of God and to share what they have with others. In this way, TD becomes a shared journey toward deeper discipleship, harmony, and Christ-likeness.

7. The church is an indispensable partner in TD work

The local church is God's chosen instrument to be both a sign and an agent of his kingdom and not simply a civil society actor or an optional development partner. Those who engage in TD have a God-given mandate to partner with the church. As Paul writes in Ephesians that it is through the church that God makes known his wisdom—even to the principalities and powers in the heavenly realms (3:10). Church partnerships vary based on context, church capacity, and local realities. In some contexts, churches actively plan and implement organized responses to poverty; in others, their efforts may be more informal and unstructured, requiring strengthening and support to engage more effectively. Yet in every circumstance, churches embody their shared calling to love God and love their neighbors. The principle remains: TD affirms and strengthens the church's presence and mission in society. Where no local church exists, frontline teams become its representative expression, and they trust that God will draw people to himself and establish his church in that place.

8. TD: Where justice and mercy meet

TD reflects the biblical mandate to "act justly, love mercy, and walk humbly with your God" (Mic 6:8). These three are not separate virtues but a unified call. Justice without mercy becomes rigid and cold. Mercy without justice becomes sentimental and ineffectual. Both virtues require humility before God, who is the source of love and justice. Throughout Scripture, justice is always tethered to righteousness, and efforts to secure justice apart from truth, holiness, and faithfulness inevitably falter. Mercy is an expression

---

11. Myers, *Walking with the Poor*, 190–202.

of how we exercise authority in situations where we hold relative power, whether through money, technical expertise, position, or influence. TD workers not only respond to immediate needs arising from poverty, pain, and exclusion, but they also engage with the deeper structural and systemic causes of injustice. TD challenges abuses of power, advocates for accountability, and promotes policies and practices that uphold dignity and equity for all, regardless of gender, caste, ethnicity, religion, age, or ability. Yet TD has a posture of humility, and it never draws attention to itself but points instead to God, whose very nature is to act justly and love mercy. TD seeks transformation at both the personal and societal levels and calls leaders to steward their power responsibly and to seek lasting change through truth and love.

9. TD requires an incarnational approach and a servant posture

At the heart of TD is the incarnational model of Jesus Christ, "the image of the invisible God," who chose to dwell among us (Col 1:15). Jesus' incarnation is a model of ministry rooted in humility, solidarity, and love; it is not merely a theological doctrine. Jesus stood with the poor, healed the brokenhearted, and proclaimed good news to the afflicted. His life and ministry reflected intimacy with the Father through the Spirit and deep engagement with the world.[12] Christian organizations and fieldworkers are called to live out this same incarnational spirituality. We do not serve from a distance. We enter into the lives of the people we serve, and we see them as made in the image of God, and we recognize them as the primary actors in their own development. We lead from demonstrations of love and servanthood and not from positions of power. Jesus came to serve, not to be served, and he calls us to do the same. Money and technical expertise alone cannot transform communities. Love, embodied, sacrificial, and faithful, is the key to lasting transformation.

10. TD is always a process

Transformational Development (TD) is a process and not a project. It is never a completed task but rather an unfolding journey that takes place in the liminal space between Christ's first coming and his promised return,

---

12. So, *Jesus' Revelation*, 207–8.

between the *already* and the *not yet* of the kingdom of God. No community, organization, or nation can claim to have fully achieved TD. We are all in process of learning, growing, and changing as we engage in God's mission. Some theologians caution against using the language of "transformation" in ways that imply human development efforts can fully realize the kingdom of God. They remind us that mission is carried out within the tension of what God has already accomplished through Christ and what he will bring to completion in the fullness of time.[13] TD must be understood within this eschatological framework. Our hope is in God's redemptive promise and not in our accomplishments. Until Christ returns, we are invited to participate faithfully in God's ongoing work of restoration; we are always dependent, always hopeful, and always unfinished.

IS TRANSFORMATIONAL DEVELOPMENT A PROJECT?

At its core, Transformational Development (TD) is God's project, and he is working to make all things new and to reconcile everything to himself through Christ. This redemptive work is ongoing and all-encompassing. But can TD also be considered the project of Christian organizations? In practice, organizations often structure their community-based work into projects and programs for the sake of management, accountability, and funding. A project is typically a time-bound intervention with clearly defined objectives, budgets, activities, and geographic focus. However, TD, as described throughout this book, is not a project in that sense. It is better understood as a set of principles, processes, and relationships. It resists rigid frameworks and standardized templates. TD emphasizes holistic transformation, something that cannot be easily confined within the limits of short-term, sector-specific projects. While specific, time-bound projects may be necessary and even helpful within the broader journey of transformation, they should not be mistaken for TD itself. TD should instead inform the vision and mission of the organization and provide a mindset and framework for how we engage with people and communities. It should guide the purpose of our work, shape the processes by which we engage, and characterize the posture and identity of the personnel doing the work on the ground. Projects may come and go, but the long, faithful journey of transformation, God's work among people, continues. As stated earlier, Christian NGO-led interventions may be referred to as

---

13. Willmer, Review of *Mission*, 195.

transformational development (lowercase) when they reflect a desire to align the work with God's ongoing redemptive mission and the ways in which he is bringing about transformation.

Purpose Beyond Projects

Transformational Development must be shaped by a holistic, kingdom-oriented vision that goes beyond meeting project targets or achieving specific outputs. TD envisions communities where people increasingly care for the vulnerable and live as agents of transformation; they embody and advance God's kingdom on earth. This deeper purpose gives meaning to the work and inspires fieldworkers to view their role as part of God's mission. Part of the TD vision is for people that we serve to become active participants in transforming their communities and to be blessed in order to be a blessing to others. Projects and programs, therefore, are not the ultimate goal; rather, they are tools, platforms, and means toward this greater vision. However, programs and projects, being time-bound and location-specific, provide the practical platform for Christian organizations to engage with the poor. These initiatives must be organized, funded, and managed. As fallen human beings, we need systems, processes, and tools to keep us focused on our mission effectively and with excellence. Yet, the challenge remains: How do we avoid losing sight of our ultimate focus? We will grapple with this major question throughout this book.

Shaping the Processes of TD

The process of engaging with the poor must be rooted in the spiritual foundation of Transformational Development (TD). The daily work of all involved should be undergirded by dependence on God as expressed through prayer, engagement with Scripture, and spiritual discernment. Rather than being shaped by short-term, time-bound project cycles, TD calls for a long-term orientation and commitment. At the heart of this process are authentic relationships with team members, community participants, and local partners that shape how fieldworkers approach their work. Yet, in the effort to implement projects and report results, there is a real danger that transformational development can become transactional development. Balancing this tension between a posture of trust and dependence on God on one hand and being faithful to project plans, while genuinely involving people in open processes on the other, remains unresolved in most organizations. This is one of the key issues we will be addressing throughout this book. To prevent transactional tendencies, fieldworkers must practice deep listening, walk alongside communities, and be willing to adjust plans based on what they discern from both God and the people they serve. This posture of openness requires flexibility, humility, and attentiveness—key virtues that ensure the process remains both faithful and responsive.

Character of the Personnel

Transformational Development requires all members of the organization to share a commitment toward a common vision of its meaning and purpose that is expressed both in organizational life and community engagement. Whether working directly in communities or serving in roles of support, leadership, or administration, all staff members are called to be growing disciples of Jesus Christ and to embody an incarnational lifestyle, loving God and loving people in tangible ways. Guided by the mindset of servanthood, they view themselves as facilitators rather than experts and approach their work with humility in a spirit of partnership. Transformational Development requires personnel to be culturally respectful, spiritually grounded, and committed to learning as much as leading. They seek wisdom from the local context and discern opportunities for growth and transformation. Personnel sustain their work through prayer, community, and a deep sense of calling to align their efforts with God's purposes, and not by technical expertise alone. Fieldworkers, as co-laborers with God, are central to the practice of transformational development. Their role as agents of holistic change, grounded in faith and community presence, will be explored throughout this book.

At the same time, we know that managers, technical leaders, and experts bring valuable skills and insights. Applying their expertise often requires a specialized approach, which can result in tension between technical efficiency and transformational processes. This book will grapple with this tension as well as explore how to integrate expertise without losing the relational and faith-driven essence of TD.

In essence, TD's vision provides the "why," its aspirations shape the "what," and its mindset forms the "how." Together, these three commitments create an environment where meaningful, faith-filled engagement with communities can occur. Within this framework, organizations take on specific projects and programs, which are part of a larger, ongoing journey of transformation that reflects both human and divine purposes.

REFLECTIVE QUESTIONS FOR PRACTITIONERS OF TRANSFORMATIONAL DEVELOPMENT

Ensuring that our understanding of TD remains holistic and grounded requires regular reflection on our practices. The principles outlined above provide a theological basis for Transformational Development—holistic, participatory, relational, and rooted in God's mission of restoration. Applying these principles in real-world settings means continually wrestling with tensions between faith and work, local realities and organizational mandates, implementing programs and relational engagement, measurable results and unseen transformation. To facilitate this ongoing process of reflection and alignment, the following questions are offered as illustrative examples. They are not an exhaustive list of questions, but are intended to highlight the need for ongoing reflection, learning, and adaptation by TD practitioners. These questions are designed to encourage fieldworkers, leaders, and partners to examine regularly the integrity of their practice and impact of their work in light of TD's core principles. Reflecting on these types of questions helps us remain mindful not to reduce the scope of TD to what can be implemented within time- and space-bound programs. Instead, it ensures that whatever we do increasingly aligns with our understanding of TD.

- How do we recognize God's work in the communities where we serve, and in what ways might we better align our efforts with his purposes?
- How do we make space for prayer, listening, and spiritual discernment in the planning and implementation of development work?
- Does our work prioritize both inward and outward changes?
- Is our engagement with people cultivating dignity, purpose, and restored identity and not just meeting physical needs?
- How do we view our roles? As experts and resource providers or as co-laborers with God and the community?
- Are local people treated as partners or as beneficiaries?

- Are we open to learning from those we serve, even when they challenge our assumptions?
- How do we ensure that the voices of marginalized people shape what we do?
- Are our interventions addressing the relational, spiritual, social, and physical dimensions of people's lives?
- Where might we be neglecting dimensions of holistic transformation?
- How has the community's engagement transformed us and our teams?
- Are our relationships marked by reciprocity and shared learning?
- How are we strengthening the local church's witness and discipleship in the community?
- Are church leaders involved as equal partners in shaping the vision?
- Are we addressing structural causes of poverty or only the symptoms?
- Do we express a healthy bias toward the most vulnerable and excluded people?
- Are we close enough to people's lives to understand their pain, dreams, and daily realities?
- Are we rushing for results or creating space for long-term transformation?
- How do we remain faithful even when outcomes are not immediately visible?

A CASE STUDY IN PRACTICE: TRANSFORMATIONAL DEVELOPMENT IN THE SACRED VALLEY, PERU

One compelling example of an NGO-led project that endeavored to put TD principles into practice comes from the Lamay district of Peru's Sacred Valley. In the early 2000s, World Vision Peru partnered with the local Richarry-Ayllu Association (RAA) to implement a series of child-focused health and development projects. This collaboration aimed to integrate holistic, community-driven approaches to improve the well-being of children and families. Over several years of visiting this district, I observed not just the outcomes of these projects but the deeper, long-term transformation that took root in the community. *Richarry-Ayllu* means

"Wake up, People!" in Quechua, which is a fitting name for a movement that sought to awaken communities to the possibilities of life in all its fullness for their children. Lamay, home to thirteen rural communities, faced significant developmental challenges at the time: low literacy rates, poor maternal and child health, widespread alcoholism, and disengaged churches. The district's Human Development Index (HDI) of 0.488 lagged far behind Peru's national average of 0.597 and underscored the urgent need for intervention.

What distinguished this initiative was not merely the particular set of health and education interventions that were introduced, but the way in which TD principles framed and guided the work. The local organization, RAA, began with a clear and deeply held vision: that their children should grow up in nurturing, value-based, God-fearing environments. This vision was rooted in the community's own hopes, spiritual convictions, and cultural identity and did not come from the outside.

A strong community-driven process supported this vision. Forty-three volunteer child promoters and maternal advisors monitored child health and development, offered family counseling, and facilitated referrals to health clinics. These volunteers became trusted figures in their communities as examples of incarnational leadership at the grassroots. They used visual tools, such as color-coded maps and charts, to track maternal and child health and foster a shared sense of responsibility and local accountability. Health monitoring centers, equipped with simple tools and educational materials, became hubs for community discussion and learning as well as for data collection.

Development planning was participatory and transparent. The community used a strategy known as the "ladder of development," which centered children's well-being as the benchmark for all progress from prenatal care to responsible parenting. Community assemblies and collaboration with district officials helped align local actions with broader development goals. This process encouraged authentic relationships, local initiative, and spiritual reflection that drew on both indigenous wisdom and biblical values. They identified the most vulnerable families and developed personalized plans to address the critical barriers each household faced—whether related to poor health, lack of access to education for children, or limited economic opportunities. Over a ten-year period, the results were remarkable: rates of child malnutrition and maternal illness dropped significantly. Alcoholism, once widespread, was eliminated. Fathers, once detached from child-rearing, began engaging with tenderness and joy, playing with their children, and supporting early childhood development. Parenting itself was transformed, with community norms now affirming nurturing care as a shared responsibility. Local churches, previously inactive and fragmented, began working together, organizing community festivals, and strengthening their witness. A renewed sense of hope began to shape how people envisioned the future.

Just as importantly, the transformation endured. Years after World Vision's external funding had ended, the communities continued to thrive. On their own initiative, they began hosting eco-tourism experiences for visitors to nearby Machu Picchu, which generated local income and sustained their development activities. The leadership capacity, rooted in a shared vision and guided by spiritual commitment, developed over time and enabled them to navigate new challenges without outside intervention.

What made this transformation possible was the presence of a clear TD purpose, participatory and relational processes, and spiritually grounded personnel. Local leaders recognized the need to change not only external conditions but also cultural practices, relationships, and values. They held a long-term vision, led by example, and chose to trust in God and in one another. They emphasized values such as justice, love, and dignity, and they reshaped family life, strengthened community cohesion, and united churches. Development was not used as a platform for evangelism, but the spiritual foundations of the community were deepened as they walked together toward transformation.

This case is just one example to show that while TD may include time-bound projects, it cannot be reduced to them. Projects can serve as platforms for transformation, but only when they are rooted in local vision, shaped by holistic processes, and led by people whose lives embody the message they seek to share. In Lamay, we see that when TD principles are lived out faithfully and the fruit endures far beyond the life of any one program.

MAPPING THE JOURNEY AHEAD

What I share here reflects my core understanding of Transformational Development and captures what I consider to be essential. This perspective has taken shape over many years through my work with Christian organizations, hands-on experience among the poor, meaningful

Introduction: Essence of Transformational Development

conversations with colleagues (especially field practitioners), and deep engagement with others' writings and reflections. I do not claim to offer a complete or exhaustive definition of TD, but I hope that reading this description at the outset will help readers understand the theological, practical, and ethical positions I take throughout the rest of this book.

This book seeks to challenge and inspire fieldworkers and organizational leaders to rethink their approaches in light of core commitments of TD, including the vital role of fieldworkers. Here is an overview of how the chapters in this book navigate key issues in pursuing holistic ministry among the poor within Christian organizations. The chapters explore how to balance organizational structure and systems with the agency of the people involved, align organizational strategy and metrics with grassroots presence, implement technically sound programs while facilitating genuine participation of vulnerable populations, and integrate external funding while recognizing community-owned resources.

This "Introduction" chapter explains TD as a holistic, God-initiated process of inside-out transformation in individuals, relationships, and systems. It highlights the important role of fieldworkers as co-laborers with God, grounded in prayer, humility, justice, and incarnational living.

The first chapter, "At the Heart of Transformation: The Role of Fieldworkers," focuses on fieldworkers' unique role as those working most directly with community members and most critical to the realization of TD. The chapter explores the expectations, challenges, and tensions fieldworkers face while navigating organizational and community realities, and it emphasizes their agency as image-bearers of God. It argues that TD is impossible without fieldworkers' full participation.

Chapter 2, "Theories of Development and the Role of Fieldworkers," explores how different theories of change—rationalistic, participatory, rights-based, and complexity-oriented—shape organizational practices and fieldworker roles. This chapter argues that a theory of change should be operational and influence everything from planning to reporting. The chapter calls for a greater alignment between TD principles and the structures that guide practice.

The third chapter, "Between Metrics and Mission: Organizational Strategy and Field Practice," unpacks how managerial logics—driven by donors, metrics, and technocratic design—affect fieldworkers' lived experience. I criticize the disconnect between TD's organizational aspirations and its actual systems of control. I also examine how to design monitoring and evaluation systems that include relational and spiritual outcomes and not just quantifiable metrics.

In chapter 4, "Evangelism and Church Partnerships Within the Context of Holistic Ministry," I reclaim the intentional witness to Christ as central to TD. The chapter criticizes the drift in many Christian NGOs toward a silent gospel or a functional separation of evangelism and development and proposes instead an incarnational and relational model of evangelism embedded in community life. The chapter concludes by exploring the potential and pitfalls of partnering with a local church.

The fifth chapter, "Framing the Fieldworkers' Role in Organizational Life," argues that TD principles must shape the Christian organization's internal life and development and not just the field practices. The chapter shows how fieldworkers' voices can be included in an organization's decision-making processes, how communities of practice can empower learning at the grassroots, and how servant leadership can reshape hierarchical culture.

The final chapter, "Catalysts of Kingdom Movements," affirms the sacredness of development work when it is rooted in God's mission, and it redefines sustainability as the ongoing work of transformational development as led by local churches and holistic practitioners. I cast a hopeful vision of fieldworkers as everyday builders of God's kingdom and conclude by calling Christian workers to live out their vocation with boldness and faithfulness.

1

At the Heart of Transformation
The Role of Fieldworkers

IN THE INTRODUCTION CHAPTER, I outlined my understanding of Transformational Development (TD) and emphasized a vision rooted in holistic change. In this chapter, I approach TD from the ground level—where the work is lived out daily—and argue that a meaningful understanding of TD requires deliberate attention to the role of fieldworkers. This chapter seeks to paint a fuller picture: Who are the fieldworkers? What role do they play? Why is their contribution so vital to TD? What challenges do they encounter? And how can organizations better support and strengthen them as they serve on the front lines?

These questions invite a broader reflection: Why focus on fieldworkers? Are they not just one part of a much larger puzzle? Are there not other actors and factors—strategic plans, funding streams, program impact, theological frameworks—that play a more significant role in shaping TD outcomes? This chapter seeks to address those questions by examining the unique and pivotal role fieldworkers play in the practice of TD. Drawing on field interviews and personal experiences, I will explain what makes their contribution so central, the challenges they face, and why their presence and posture matters so deeply to the development outcomes undertaken by Christians with a missional intent.

Development, at its core, is a profoundly human endeavor that depends on qualities such as commitment, motivation, identity, trust, and relational intelligence. Development workers must be willing to collaborate with individuals, families, and communities. In TD, these human dimensions are inseparable from the spiritual aspects of life. Religious beliefs, values, and worldviews deeply influence behavior, relationships, and community change. While secular, modernist approaches to development often treat faith as irrelevant, private, or merely auxiliary, TD recognizes spirituality and faith as essential to its framework and practice. Meaningful development, especially when it seeks transformation, requires time, trust, dialogue, learning, sacrifice, and deep engagement, which are nurtured through the daily, relational work of fieldworkers. Despite the rise of global strategies, evidence-based best practices, and digital tools, the value of grounded, human engagement remains irreplaceable. Fieldworkers embody that engagement because they not only implement programs but also serve as bridge-builders, interpreters, witnesses, and companions in the journey of transformation.

THE FIELDWORKERS—TD'S HANDS AND FEET

Fieldworkers are those who serve directly in the communities that an organization is called to serve. They are, quite literally, an organization's hands and feet working among people in poverty. Positioned at the front lines (and often at the lowest tier of the organizational hierarchy), fieldworkers carry out daily, relational work that is both personal, programmatic, and profoundly impactful. They are commonly referred to by various titles, including Community Development Workers, Field Coordinators, and, when specialized, as Agricultural Extension Workers, Community Health Facilitators, or technical designations. Depending on the context and organization, they may also be known as Social Mobilizers, Community Liaison Officers, or Field Technicians. Fieldworkers engage regularly with individuals and families on issues that may be invisible from a distance: beliefs, motivation, identity, confidence, and hope. No matter how compelling an organization's mission, how strategic its plans, or how abundant its resources, the quality and integrity of its contribution to Transformational Development ultimately rests on the shoulders of fieldworkers. Whether part of international NGOs,[1] local NGOs, churches,

---

1. Many international NGOs, such as Tearfund and Christian Aid, primarily partner with local NGOs, churches, or community-based organizations to implement their programs. Others, such as World Vision and Compassion International, typically coordinate

community-based organizations, or mission agencies, these individuals carry out the vision where it matters most—on the ground.

Fieldworkers come from many roles and backgrounds: they may be health workers, teachers, agricultural extension agents, early childhood caregivers, community facilitators, evangelists, missionaries, or church workers. Some are community volunteers; others earn salaries as staff members. Many personnel come from the very communities they serve or from nearby regions so they share the peoples' language, culture, and traditions.[2] Their local knowledge and cultural competence make them indispensable in building trust and navigating complex grassroots engagement. Without fieldworkers, community-level work would be irregular at best. Although one-off activities can be supported remotely, any meaningful, sustained engagement—particularly the kind of ongoing, trust-based presence that reflects the principles of TD—would be nearly impossible. It is fieldworkers who carry the organization's mission, vision, and strategy into the daily lives of communities. While advocacy work, such as policy influence, coalition building, or public campaigning, can be led at the national or regional level, even these efforts often rest on the credibility and outcomes of micro-level work accomplished by field teams.

WHO THEY ARE AND WHAT THEY DO

At the grassroots, fieldworkers nurture relationships, encourage participation, guide planning and implementation, raise awareness, provide education, manage micro-loans, monitor progress, and report outcomes—the list is long and vital. In essence, fieldworkers are responsible for delivering much of an organization's mission and programming to local communities. Their essential roles have been described in many ways. They are facilitators, change agents, gatekeepers, technical experts, relational brokers, and even "street-level bureaucrats." Fieldworkers have been criticized, though, as modernizing disrupters of tradition and as agents of foreign values and interests. These tensions reflect their complex position.

---

program design and implementation through their own nationally registered offices, while also engaging local actors in various roles.

2. Only in rare cases, such as Peace Corps or missionary-sending organizations, do fieldworkers happen to be foreigners. Such foreign fieldworkers are usually based in local communities for a limited period of time so they can gain experience and legitimacy. After being in the field at the beginning of their professional careers, they tend to move to other kinds of roles. This book will not address the issues faced by such expatriate staff.

Whatever the label, their presence, posture, and performance are crucial to whether TD takes root and flourishes at the local level.

Observers and practitioners have long acknowledged the pivotal role of fieldworkers at the intersection of development organizations and communities.[3] Fieldworkers live out the organization's mission, vision, and values, while also planning and implementing programs on its behalf. They are expected not only to deliver services but also to serve as custodians of the feedback loop and to ensure that the hopes, insights, and aspirations of the communities are communicated upward and then are meaningfully reflected in organizational strategies and plans.

Despite widespread recognition of the transformative nature of their work, development studies have paid surprisingly little attention to fieldworkers' lived experiences, roles, and perspectives. Their contributions, especially in the context of developing countries, remain largely unexplored and undervalued.[4] While fieldworkers often occupy the lowest rung in organizational hierarchies, they are, in fact, in a critical position where they can either advance or undermine the mission and effectiveness of their organizations. This dependence on frontline staff is aptly captured by Alan Fowler in the following statement:

> Defining the roles and competencies of change agents is vital for their effective development. Getting this wrong, regardless of how well everything else is done, sustainable development will not be likely.[5]

Origins of Fieldworkers in Community-Based Development Work

The role of fieldworkers or change agents in community development has its roots in the long history of cross-cultural Christian missions. Early Catholic missionary practices such as *inculturation*, in which missionaries adapted themselves to the cultures they entered, and Protestant efforts at *vernacularization*, particularly the translation of Scripture from Latin into local languages, were intentional strategies of cultural engagement. These approaches use familiar cultural forms to communicate the gospel in accessible and meaningful ways to ordinary people. Such practices,

---

3. Taylor and Jenkins, *Time to Listen*, 1–2.
4. Ahmad, "Bearers of Change," 177; Fechter and Hindman, *Everyday Lives*, 5.
5. Fowler, *Striking a Balance*, 60.

and the relational engagement they signified, did more than facilitate the spread of the Christian faith. Their work required long-term presence, cultural competence, and deep relational engagement—qualities that modern development practice now recognizes as essential. Although Christian missions have not been without critique, they demonstrated that transformation requires presence. Missionaries lived among the people they served, engaging not only spiritual needs but also educational, health, and social realities. In doing so, they laid a foundation for much of what today's development practitioners describe as holistic, participatory, and community led.[6] The legacy of mission work is complex and sometimes troubling, especially where it was entangled with European colonial expansion or where it perpetuated cultural domination. While critiques of these actions are valid and important, they are not directly relevant to our discussions here.

The example of Christian missions demonstrates a fundamental principle: any effort to influence people's beliefs, values, relationships, and behaviors requires sustained, in-depth engagement with their social and cultural realities. Christian missionaries, despite their flaws, have been involved in this kind of grassroots engagement for centuries. Their work shows that community transformation cannot happen at a distance but must be incarnational, relational, and contextually grounded. These principles remain central to the role of fieldworkers in TD today.

The Rise of Fieldworkers in Participatory Development

In the late 1960s and 1970s, the idea of community-based fieldworkers who facilitated development at the grassroots level became integral to the emerging discourse on participatory development. The terms *participation* and *participatory* entered the development lexicon during this period, largely as a reaction to the failure of top-down, donor-funded strategies centered on industrialization and large-scale infrastructure projects that had followed the decolonization of many developing nations. With the emergence of neoliberal policies—represented in the Washington Consensus and favoring market-driven economies and a reduced role for the state, governments began to withdraw from rural development. In this vacuum, NGOs captured the opportunity to promote alternative, community-based approaches that emphasized indigenous knowledge,

---

6. Robert, *Christian Mission*, 38.

local engagement, and participatory decision-making.[7] As a result, a wide range of participatory methodologies began to take shape in the 1980s and beyond; these efforts sought to place people at the center of development processes.

The Freirean Legacy and the Role of the "Animator"

A key intellectual influence on this movement toward a participatory approach was Paulo Freire, whose foundational works *Pedagogy of the Oppressed* (1970) and *Education for Critical Consciousness* (1974) argued that the poor and marginalized should be enabled to analyze critically their own realities and initiate their own liberation. Freire's model emphasizes dialogical action, through which oppressed people can develop a critical consciousness (*conscientização*) of their social condition.[8] The educator or "animator," as it was often termed in development practice, does not provide solutions but rather accompanies people in a process of reflection and collective action. This Freirean understanding of community facilitation has had a lasting impact on grassroots development. In Sri Lanka, for example, a program rooted in Freire's philosophy explains how it works:

> The role of the animator (community facilitator, change agent, catalyst, or activist as variously called) is a central factor in the generation of self-reliant grassroots initiatives. The essence of this role is a catalytic one of stimulating the rural poor to a systematic reflection of the causal factors in their poverty and deprivation and of assisting them to realize their self-reliant potential through their own organized efforts.[9]

This program description highlights the importance of fieldworkers' agency; their ability to catalyze, accompany, and learn with communities is essential to local ownership and sustainable change.

The emergence of fieldworkers in both secular and faith-based traditions points to a shared recognition: that real change is local, relational, and deeply human. Whether called facilitators, animators, community health workers, or missionaries, these individuals play a pivotal mediating role between institutions and communities; they walk alongside people

---

7. Mosse, *Cultivating Development*, 21.
8. Freire, *Pedagogy of the Oppressed*, 47–9.
9. Tilakaratna, "Animator," i.

as they journey toward transformation. What modern development has formalized in programming policy, Christian mission previously practiced as calling. Together, these practices affirm that development cannot be delivered from a distance. It must be lived and sustained through presence.

Participation, Power, and the Expansion of Fieldworker Roles

Coinciding with Freire and changes in participatory development, field-level engagement also became central in public health following the 1978 Alma-Ata Declaration. At that time, the World Health Organization began promoting Community Health Workers (CHWs) as the cornerstone of its "Health for All by the Year 2000" strategy. CHWs were envisioned as a bridge between formal healthcare systems and remote or underserved populations. Though not medically trained professionals, CHWs provided health education, facilitated vaccination campaigns, promoted disease prevention, and collected local health data.[10] CHWs, like community development fieldworkers, relied on trust, relational presence, and local cultural knowledge, which underscored the irreplaceable value of embedded, grassroots personnel.

EXPECTATIONS FOR FIELDWORKERS

Having explored the emergence of the fieldworker role in history and practice, we turn now to examine some common work-related expectations for fieldworkers engaged in community development. What follows is a generic profile of a fieldworker's roles and responsibilities in organizations doing community-based TD work. While the list may vary depending on the organization's sectoral focus (e.g., health, agriculture, education, etc.), the core principles and competencies described here remain broadly applicable across contexts.

Community-Facing Responsibilities

Fieldworkers engaged in community-based development carry a combination of strategic, relational, and operational responsibilities. At a strategic level, they act as the community-facing voice of the organization,

---

10. Medcalf and Nunes, "Primary Health Care," 401–24.

communicating its identity, mission, vision, values, and holistic approach to development. They are expected to develop a deep understanding of the local context, including government plans, cultural dynamics, and community priorities, and to ensure that the concerns of all groups, especially the marginalized, are heard and respected. Building trust-based relationships with community leaders and members are foundational to their work, as is fostering collaboration among local stakeholders, partners, and external actors. Fieldworkers also identify and engage with local churches and faith-based organizations to nurture active partnerships that share values and contribute to the spiritual, social, and physical well-being of communities.

At an operational level, fieldworkers facilitate and support key community meetings and workshops, coordinate with technical experts to implement program activities, and raise awareness within local communities on specific development issues. Fieldworkers endeavor to build the capacity of local partners and community groups, advocate on behalf of people they serve with service providers (e.g., schools, clinics, agricultural offices), and handle local logistics for trainings, events, and supplies. Detailed planning, close coordination with stakeholders, and regular monitoring of activities are essential aspects of their role. Fieldworkers need to remain flexible and take corrective action as needed, and at the same time they live out the organization's faith and values through their presence, relationships, and day-to-day service. In both strategy and implementation, fieldworkers play a critical role in ensuring that the organization's mission becomes a lived reality at the grassroots level.

Organization-Facing Responsibilities

In addition to their community-facing roles, fieldworkers also serve as a critical bridge between the grassroots and the organization they represent. Fieldworkers communicate the local context, needs, and opportunities to management. They help ensure that organizational plans remain relevant and responsive, and they contribute to local-level planning within the organization's frameworks and guidelines. In addition to providing feedback based on their real-time insights from the field, fieldworkers regularly collect data, prepare reports, explain any deviations from agreed targets or timelines, and justify any over- or under-spending of the budget. When local realities shift, fieldworkers may need to advocate for changes to previously developed plans and provide the rationale and evidence needed to inform adaptive management.

Fieldworkers also play a key role in supporting the organization's external communication and donor engagement efforts. They gather and share stories, photographs, and other media that are tailored to different donor expectations in order to illustrate progress and impact. In many cases, fieldworkers also conduct surveys and other data collection exercises to support organizational learning and accountability. Internally, fieldworkers respond to regular queries from management, participate in organizational trainings and planning meetings, and contribute to institutional processes. They are often responsible for coordinating and hosting organizational visitors including donors, and they ensure that visits are meaningful, culturally appropriate, and reflective of both the organization's values and the community's dignity. Through all of these responsibilities, fieldworkers not only implement but actively represent the organization; they shape how it is perceived both within and beyond the communities it serves.

Taken together, these community- and organization-facing responsibilities reveal that fieldworkers are far more than program implementers. They are foot soldiers, relational bridges, and cultural interpreters. Their faithfulness, discernment, and integrity profoundly shape not only how programs function on the ground but how the mission of TD is embodied and made credible in the lives of those they serve.

Organizational Discourse, Culture, and Fieldworker Expectations

The expectations outlined above reflect only the formal dimensions of a fieldworker's role that are typically captured in job descriptions and performance frameworks. However, the actual experience of fieldwork is not defined solely by policy documents or stated objectives. It is shaped just as much, if not more, by the organization's culture and discourse as revealed in the day-to-day practices, relational dynamics, and planning and management systems that frame how work gets done. These cultural patterns create the lived environment within which fieldworkers interpret and enact their responsibilities. Consider, for example, how an organization's core values influence its internal discourse and, in turn, fieldworker behavior. Most organizations articulate a set of core values, but the real question is whether those values function as reference points in organizational life. Do they guide decision-making in moments of strategic, operational, or ethical tension? Do they meaningfully shape the attitudes, behaviors, and interactions of leaders, staff, and volunteers? If so, then these values become part of the organizational discourse and form a powerful system of meaning that influences how fieldworkers internalize their roles, make choices, and relate to the communities they serve. If core values do not shape behavior, then the actual values, as seen in daily behavior, informal conversations, and unspoken expectations, will take their place and shape field practice. The same principle applies to mission statements, strategic plans, workplace policies, and program frameworks: their real influence depends not on how they are written but on how they are lived out and enforced. They have a direct influence on how fieldworkers understand and carry out their roles.

Another example of how an organization's values affect fieldworkers is in its discourse on risk aversion, especially in contexts where maintaining donor trust, public reputation, or compliance with safeguarding policies is paramount. While risk management is necessary, an overly cautious organizational culture can lead to hyper-regulation of field activities, which limits fieldworkers' ability to respond flexibly to emerging needs. For example, a fieldworker may identify a promising grassroots initiative or a spontaneous opportunity for a pilot project, but they hesitate to act because of the organization's approval and budgeting process. In such cases, innovation and responsiveness can be stifled by fear of deviation from protocol or violating unwritten rules. When risk-aversion becomes a dominant narrative, it shapes field-level behavior, and it prioritizes safety, control, and predictability over experimentation, contextual responsiveness, or relational boldness. Over time, these lived values can diminish the very agency and creativity needed for transformational development to take root.

Fieldworkers and Their Work Contexts in Communities

Fieldworkers are typically based in or near the communities they serve, rather than in organizational headquarters or regional offices. As a result, their day-to-day work environment is markedly different from that of their managers and all other staff based who work in institutional settings or remotely from the comfort of their homes. This physical and organizational distance creates a contextual divide: fieldworkers may not fully understand the broader organizational pressures their managers face, whether from donors, government partners, or NGO global headquarters. They are keenly aware, though, of the expectations placed directly on them.

Unless fieldworkers originally come from the communities in which they work, a social and cultural distance may also exist between them and the local population, especially in the early years. While fieldworkers may see themselves as junior staff or technical personnel, community members often perceive them as representatives of powerful organizations, who have access to financial resources, influential networks, and valuable information. A community's perception can amplify expectations and shape how communities interact with fieldworkers.

Because they live and work among the people, fieldworkers encounter firsthand the complex realities of community life. They witness both deep needs and untapped opportunities, navigate interpersonal tensions, and are often drawn into local conflicts that arise during program implementation. In some cases, they may become entangled, consciously or not, in the agendas of local elites who wish to benefit from organizational programs. These elites may attempt to influence the fieldworker's actions, or, conversely, fieldworkers may leverage their influence to expedite projects or resolve disputes.

While fieldworkers develop an intimate familiarity with the communities they serve, this embeddedness can be both an asset and a limitation. As the anonymous saying goes, "We don't know who discovered water, but it wasn't the fish." Similarly, individuals deeply immersed in a context may struggle to see it with objectivity. The same closeness that fosters trust and insight can also obscure broader patterns or power dynamics. Thus, while fieldworkers often understand their communities better than anyone else in the organization, their interpretations are shaped by their own positionality—something both they and their organizations must continually reflect upon.

AGENCY IN DEVELOPMENT

Given the embedded and often complex realities that fieldworkers navigate, it is essential to consider the role of agency, both within the communities they serve and within the fieldworkers themselves. A foundational belief in community development is that people should be agents of their own development, not passive recipients of external interventions. Outsiders, whether organizations or field staff, are meant to play supportive and facilitative roles, rather than directive or controlling ones. But what does it truly mean to be an agent of one's own development? British sociologist Anthony Giddens describes human beings as purposive agents, who are capable of shaping their actions in pursuit of particular goals.[11] According to Giddens, agency consists of two key elements: knowledgeability (the ability to understand one's context and possibilities) and capability (the freedom and capacity to make choices and act on them).[12] Agency implies more than participation: it implies power, intention, and action. To be an agent is to act with purpose and the freedom to move toward one's chosen ends. Agents possess values as well as the reflective capacity to align their actions with their beliefs.[13]

In this sense, agency is not compatible with being a mere functionary in a standardized process. An agent is not simply a tool used by others to achieve predetermined outcomes but someone who acts freely and meaningfully within a given context. Giddens's structuration theory explains that social structures both shape individual actions and are shaped by the same actions. There is a constant interplay between structure and agency, with individuals influencing the systems they inhabit, even as those systems shape the possibilities available to them.

In the field of development, the agency of both community members and fieldworkers should be considered as they influence and are influenced by each other. Both are part of the social systems they seek to transform, and both can exercise influence through intentional, collective action. For Christian organizations engaged in Transformational Development, fieldworker agency is essential. It is difficult, perhaps impossible, to empower communities to act as agents of their own change while simultaneously denying that same agency to the individuals who accompany them. To expect fieldworkers to facilitate deep, context-sensitive transformation without granting them the space to adapt, reflect, and act meaningfully is to undermine the very model of development such organizations claim to support. If agency is to be upheld as a core principle in development, it must be practiced and protected, not just among those served but among those who serve.

---

11. Giddens, *Constitution of Society*, 3.
12. Giddens, *Constitution of Society*, 90–96.
13. Frie, *Psychological Agency*, 51.

Foundation for Agency: Bearing the Image of God

The foundational verses for understanding agency in a biblical context are in Gen 1:26–27, which declare human beings as created in the image and likeness of God. These verses have been interpreted in diverse ways throughout Christian history.[14] Middleton provides a helpful survey of these interpretations, highlighting several dimensions of what it means to bear God's image: the capacity to reason, the ethical ability to respond obediently to God, the capacity for relationships, and the unique human vocation to represent God's rule within creation.[15] Central to the biblical narrative is the idea that God grants agency and freedom to human beings—not only the capacity to relate and reason but also the freedom to resist, disobey, or choose.[16] Because humans bear God's image, they possess inherent dignity, worth, and value, that cannot be earned by status or achievement but are bestowed by God.[17] This theological foundation affirms the basic equality of all people, regardless of social class, gender, ethnicity, or ability. Those who are socially marginalized or considered of lower status do not need to define themselves through the distorted lenses of those who hold power over them. Rather, their identity and worth are grounded in their Creator. This understanding compels us to treat others with care, respect, and mutual concern. As Jack Mahoney observes, being made in God's image invites us into a life of neighbor-love, other-centeredness, and shared responsibility for one another's well-being.[18]

The implications of the imago Dei for development work are profound. To be created in God's image is to be a co-creator with God, endowed with the ability to observe, reason, and act for the common good.[19] Human beings do not passively receive development, but they are purposeful actors, entrusted with gifts and responsibilities for the flourishing of others. This theological affirmation of human agency and vocation forms the very foundation of Transformational Development. For Christian organizations, this has direct implications not only for how they engage communities, but also for how they view and support fieldworkers. Fieldworkers' agency and

14. Grenz, *Social God*, 19–26.
15. Middleton, *Liberating Image*, 19–26.
16. Middleton, *Liberating Image*, 289.
17. Kilner, *Dignity and Destiny*, 250–51.
18. Mahoney, "Evolution, Altruism, and the Image," 701.
19. Myers, *Walking with the Poor*, 61.

calling must be honored just as much as that of the communities they serve. As Bryant Myers reminds us, perhaps the most important thing a Christian development worker can do is to be fully present—with God and with the poor—not as one in control, but as one open to what God is doing and what may yet unfold.[20] Recognizing the image of God in both the served and the servant reframes development as a shared journey of transformation that is rooted in mutual dignity, vocation, and trust.

FIELDWORKER AGENCY IN DEVELOPMENT PRACTICE

At its core, development is a deeply relational and social process involving people in families, communities, and institutions who learn how to care for and collaborate with one another for the common good. Within this framework, the agency of fieldworkers becomes central to development for two key reasons. First, no matter how meticulously a program is designed, development is inherently adaptive. Each context is unique, requiring field-level discretion, judgment, and responsiveness. Fieldworkers often encounter situations that fall outside the formal scope of project plans yet demand real-time decisions for meaningful progress. The contexts in which planning occurs do not remain static: by the time implementation begins, contexts change. Second, development is not solely about structured activities and predetermined outputs. Projects unfold through ongoing learning, open dialogue, and trust-based relationships that emerge over time—elements that cannot be captured through traditional planning or management tools. For these two reasons, fieldworkers do not merely implement projects; they become agents of change who navigate complexity and respond to emerging realities with creativity and discernment.

While the practice of affirming fieldworker agency remains limited in many organizational structures, its importance has been acknowledged in select scholarly works. As early as the 1960s, Albert Hirschman's study of eleven long-term World Bank development projects sought to understand what explained their varying outcomes. He introduced what he called the "principle of the hiding hand."[21] Hirschman observed that successful projects often encountered unexpected obstacles during implementation but also benefited from equally unexpected creative responses by those working on the ground. These "remedial actions," typically taken by local

20. Myers, *Walking with the Poor*, 233.
21. Hirschman, *Development Projects Observed*, 11–14.

actors, were rarely foreseen at the planning stage. He argued that the need for creativity of those engaged in the field was underestimated in the original project designs. He wrote:

> Creativity always comes as a surprise to us; therefore, we can never count on it; and dare not believe until it has happened.[22]

Hirschman's insight underscores an important truth: the need for field-level creativity cannot be fully anticipated, scripted, or controlled. Neither can it be ignored. Fieldworkers themselves may not recognize their full capacity for creative action until they are confronted with real-world challenges or opportunities. Just as it is difficult to foresee how community contexts will evolve, it is equally difficult to prescribe in advance how fieldworkers should respond. What becomes essential, then, is creating space for fieldworkers to exercise agency and to respond authentically, intelligently, and ethically within dynamic and complex environments.

Qualities That Strengthen Fieldworker Agency

A number of scholars have emphasized that effective fieldwork is not simply about technical competence, but it is about the attitudes, character, and behaviors that allow fieldworkers to exercise their agency meaningfully—even if their organizational plan does not explicitly highlight their own agency in development work. Bryant Myers notes that if transformational development is about transforming relationships, fieldworkers must embody the right attitudes and mindsets. They must live out the very principles of transformation in how they relate to others—building trust, listening deeply, and approaching their work with humility and professionalism.[23] Similarly, Alan Fowler emphasizes character traits such as patience, empathy, perseverance, diplomacy, and respectfulness, alongside communication, negotiation, and contextual analysis skills. He stresses that effective fieldworkers need a deep understanding of the communities they serve—something that cannot be taught in a classroom or manual, but must be cultivated over time.[24]

---

22. Hirschman, *Development Projects Observed*, 13.
23. Myers, *Walking with the Poor*, 221–26.
24. Fowler, *Striking a Balance*, 84.

Robert Chambers also calls attention to what he terms the "primacy of the personal" in his article by the same title.[25] In his view, development is always mediated through individual choices. Policy and performance are not abstract systems—they are enacted through what people personally choose to do or not do. Chambers writes:

> This is the fact that individual personal choice of what to do and how to do it mediates every action and every change. Policy, practice, and performance are all outcomes of personal actions. What is done or not done depends on what people choose to do and not to do.[26]

Chambers's emphasis on personal values is particularly critical when fieldworkers enter marginalized communities as outsiders. He warns that development professionals—whom he calls "uppers"—often seek credibility, power, and influence in their interactions with the "lowers." This creates a barrier to understanding the lived realities of the poor. He calls for a reversal of attitudes: a willingness to disempower oneself, hand over discretion to others, encourage local initiative, and foster genuine community participation.[27]

This posture of humility and empowerment requires personal resolve. Fieldworkers must choose to create space, form alliances, and act with vision and courage to make change possible, even within the constraints of their institutional settings.[28] Celayne Heaton-Shrestha observes that fieldworkers from urban, educated, middle-class backgrounds must learn to adapt their speech, attitudes, and behavior, and to shed professional biases and other symbols of power in order to work effectively with marginalized communities.[29]

Together, these scholars highlight the critical role of fieldworkers' attitudes, character, and behaviors in their exercise of agency. For these qualities to be sustained, they must flow from the fieldworkers' own agency rather than being externally imposed. Fieldworker agency is not an optional enhancement; it is a cornerstone of effective and ethical development practice. When organizations recognize this reality by creating the conditions for field-level initiative, learning, and relational integrity, their

---

25. Chambers, "Primacy of the Personal," 241–53.
26. Chambers, "Primacy of the Personal," 246.
27. Chambers, *Whose Reality Counts?*, 32.
28. Chambers, "Primacy of the Personal," 247.
29. Heaton-Shrestha, "Ambiguities of Practising," 39–63.

actions align more closely with the spirit of Transformational Development. When organizations fail to cultivate fieldworkers' agency, they risk turning fieldworkers into passive implementers of plans, which, no matter how well designed, can never fully account for the dynamism, complexity, and potential of human lives.

Agency in Externally Initiated Interventions and Accountability in Development

Community and fieldworker participation and agency are central TD. But some resources come from outside the community, for example, valuable technical knowledge and resources. These external resources, when rightly applied, can significantly enhance people's well-being. In order to integrate effectively such resources and to manage the inherent complexities of community development, work is often structured into programs, projects, and activities. These categories provide a framework for management, accountability, and resource allocation. External expertise and evidence-based interventions may be indispensable, depending on an initiative's objectives. Not every community needs to reinvent solutions to known problems. For example, we have a strong body of knowledge on how to reduce maternal and child mortality, improve crop yields, teach foundational literacy, or extend micro-credit to women entrepreneurs. These interventions are based on extensive research and practical application, and they represent some of the best knowledge available to us as human beings.

As Christian development practitioners, we have a responsibility to offer the best of what we know—to steward well the insights, tools, and evidence available for others' flourishing. But this raises important questions: What is the role of community agency and fieldworker discretion when working with proven, externally developed solutions? How do we discern when external inputs are needed or when locally generated solutions may be more appropriate? More crucially, how can we introduce evidence-based practices without diminishing the initiative, ownership, and agency of both the people we serve and those who work alongside them? While integration of external practices and internal initiatives is possible in theory, the practice of development in many organizations, including Christian ones, has increasingly tilted toward a model where development is framed as a series of externally initiated interventions. These are often funded by outside donors, bound to specific timelines, and shaped by problem-solving approaches that divide complex, holistic realities into discrete sectors or disciplines. Such models emphasize technical soundness, standardization, and performance management. The project frameworks prioritize measurable outputs and best practices, but often at the expense of local participation, community ownership, and the fieldworkers' discretion.

Although this externally based approach may not explicitly deny the importance of agency, it tends to reduce community/fieldworker agency to being a means toward pre-defined ends, rather than a value in itself. People's participation becomes instrumental—a box to be checked or a tool for efficiency—rather than an expression of dignity, voice, or calling. Fieldworkers, in turn, are often treated as implementers of external logic models, rather than as reflective practitioners, cultural interpreters, or co-laborers in God's mission. This dynamic creates deep tensions for fieldworkers, especially when donor-driven accountability frameworks conflict with the lived realities, priorities, and relational rhythms of the communities they serve.

These tensions are not easily resolved, and they raise significant theological, ethical, and practical questions for the future of TD. While a more detailed exploration will follow in a later chapter, it is important to note here that fieldworker agency must not be sidelined, even in programs that are highly structured or technically oriented. When the development process neglects the agency of people at the front lines, it risks becoming efficient but hollow, technically sound but relationally impoverished.

FIELDWORKER TENSIONS IN PROGRAMS FOCUSED ON TD

When fieldworkers are positioned at the intersection of managerial approaches that are based on technical imperatives and community realities, the tensions between competing development paradigms become starkly visible. Most organizations, including Christian NGOs, simultaneously draw on multiple models of development, often without acknowledging or reconciling their underlying contradictions. The fieldworker who operates at this interface becomes the point of convergence where these tensions arise. The managerial approaches emphasize structured planning, predictability, technical imperatives, and control. Development is framed as a set of interventions designed to produce measurable outcomes, supported by management systems that ensure accountability to donors. By contrast, TD envisions change as relational, contextually grounded, and spiritually informed. It prioritizes participation, emergence, and local agency over linear logic and standardized solutions.

The tension between these divergent approaches produces what Wallace et al. describe as a conflict of discourses. Organizations and their donors often promote participatory approaches, and affirm the value of grassroots ownership; at the same time, they insist on the delivery of predetermined results based on evidence-based best practices.[30] Organizations and donors may frame these paradigms as complementary, but they are frequently in tension, both conceptually and practically. Fieldworkers must manage this unresolved duality: to ensure genuine participation, facilitate learning processes, and establish community ownership, while also delivering fixed targets and timelines. The result is more than operational complexity—it becomes a moral and ethical dilemma. Fieldworkers find themselves caught between honoring the agency of the people they serve and complying with reporting systems that reduce participation to meeting predefined metrics.

For Christian organizations, this conflict carries theological weight. Participation is not just a programmatic strategy; it reflects a deeper belief in human dignity and agency that lies at the heart of an understanding of TD. Yet these same organizations, like their secular counterparts, rely heavily on managerial tools, performance metrics, and donor reporting frameworks. TD may influence how Christian NGOs articulate their mission and community engagement, but its implications for organizational structures, systems, policies, and management practices remain underdeveloped. As a result, fieldworkers operate within systems that affirm the language of transformation but often default to the practices of control.

The accompanying diagram (see below) visualizes this tension. It contrasts two dominant paradigms shaping the fieldworker's environment. On the right is the participatory, relational, and emergent approach rooted in the values of transformational development. On the left is the technical, managerial, and performance-driven approach shaped by organizational accountability systems. Fieldworkers stand in the middle, expected to integrate and operationalize both, often without adequate support or structural alignment.

---

30. Wallace et al., *Aid Chain*, 3.

Diagram 1.1—Fieldworker Tension

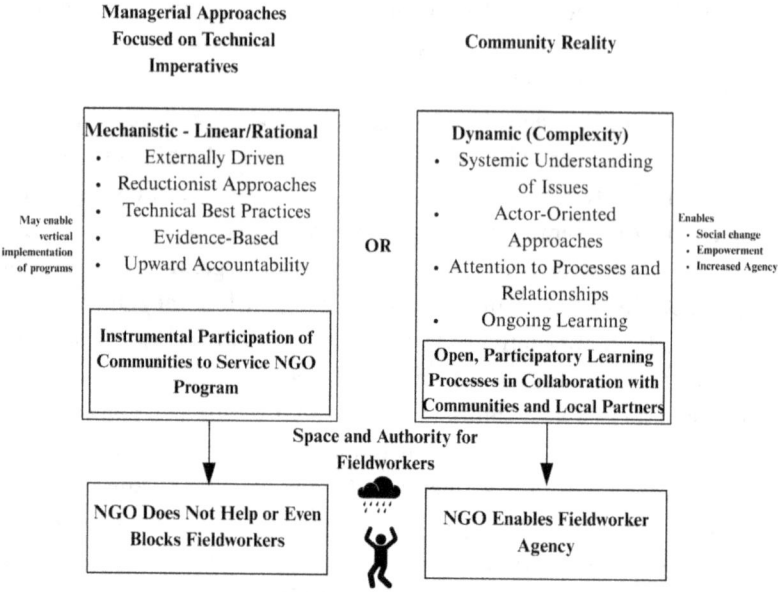

INTRODUCTION TO THE DEVELOPMENT WORKER PROFILES

To ground the discussion of fieldworker agency in lived experience, I present the profiles of five real development workers I encountered in diverse contexts—some through field research in 2018, others through collaborative work in the field during the early 2000s, and some more recently in the 2020s. Their stories reflect a range of organizational and ministry settings and reveal the different ways calling, character, and agency are lived out in practice. Together, these profiles offer a vivid picture of how transformational development unfolds across varied environments and the ways fieldworkers must draw on creativity, resilience, and deep faithfulness amid complex realities.

Development Worker Profile One—Called Like Moses

At forty-three years old and with more than sixteen years of experience as a Community Development Worker, Moses held degrees in both economics and theology. Although recently assigned to a new program, his commitment remained unwavering. His wife and two children lived in their hometown, some five hundred kilometers away, and he visited them twice a month. Moses made this sacrifice to protect their stability and education.

He saw his work as a direct calling from God: just as Moses was called to set his people free, he believed he was called to "lead his people go out of poverty." His faith deeply shaped his sense of responsibility, and he was often moved to tears when he witnessed suffering. After a tragic suicide of a family due to hunger, he reflected that God might one day ask him, *"You were there—why didn't you act?"*

Managing ten communities with a population of over ten thousand, he lived a disciplined, prayerful life and spent long days visiting villages and working weekends. Moses' commitment was rooted in a profound personal conviction that he had been chosen for this role, which motivated him to persevere despite the difficulties he encounters. Moses was resilient in navigating complex program requirements, such as pursing organizational targets that were assigned to him or collaborating with government partners who might not always meet their commitments. He felt a personal responsibility to act and make a difference whenever he encountered families that struggled to survive. While program targets were necessary for measuring success, he felt that the focus on numbers sometimes detracted him from pursuing meaningful transformation. This tension became especially evident whenever community members expressed dissatisfaction, particularly around the lack of direct assistance to them. He also found it difficult when families accused him of exploiting their stories without delivering help, highlighting the moral and ethical dilemmas inherent in his role.

Three months after I met him, he was tragically killed in an auto accident while visiting a community, a sobering reminder of the dangers fieldworkers face in their faithful service.

Development Worker Profile Two—Loyal Like Ruth

A thirty-seven-year-old with a postgraduate degree in social work, Ruth began her journey as an intern and rose to become a seasoned fieldworker over twelve years. Supported by her strong Christian faith and family network, she lived apart from her husband and children during the week and visited them on weekends. It was a difficult arrangement that weighed on her, but she accepted it as necessary.

When I met Ruth, she was responsible for seventeen villages and more than ten thousand people, and she typically worked ten to twelve hours a day. She believes that transformational development work cannot fit into an eight-hour schedule. Early challenges in building trust with communities eventually gave way to deep relationships. She takes pride in knowing the more than five hundred children in her program area by name. For her, development work has become not just a duty but a joyful partnership with the communities she serves.

Ruth demonstrates resilience and dedication in her role, managing to balance community engagement with organizational expectations. Her stable family situation allows her to invest significant time in community work, including evening visits, which she views as a positive aspect of her work. She shows strong commitment to community ownership, emphasizing that her role is to support communities in taking initiative rather than implementing programs herself. Additionally, her background in nutrition helps her effectively address community health challenges, particularly counseling for pregnant mothers and malnutrition among children. Ruth experiences guilt about past family decisions, particularly regarding the time spent away from her children when they were young. Balancing community engagement with organizational targets is a recurring challenge, as some targets are difficult to meet due to community realities, like mobilizing men for programs. The organizational directive to shift from personal interactions to capture monitoring data to mobile-based monitoring has created a disconnect, reducing the face-to-face contact Ruth values. Moreover, navigating the pressure from organizational hierarchy while maintaining accurate data and meeting the reporting demands adds stress to her role and reduces community engagement, which she considers to be central to her role.

Development Worker Profile Three—Playful Sokchean

Beginning at just twenty-four years old, Sokchean brought vibrant energy and hands-on skills to his role. Although young, he joined the program with four years of experience under his belt. Drawing on his vocational school diploma in agriculture, he led food security programs across fifteen villages and demonstrated practices like green manuring, composting, and integrated fish farming. He lives simply and dedicates most of his waking hours to farmers and their families. He engages children in playful learning activities and ensures that villagers' voices are reflected in all program decisions. Sokchean's journey as a fieldworker has been shaped by both his personal faith and his commitment to his community. Coming from a different faith background, his decision to embrace Christianity brought challenges within his family, straining his relationships with his parents. Despite this personal cost, Sokchean found a deeper sense of calling through his newfound faith, which strengthened his commitment to the people he serves.

Due to his limited English skills and discomfort with technology, Sokchean often feels out of place in formal office settings. He perceives himself as inferior to his colleagues, who appear more sophisticated in their speech, manners, and attire. Sokchean's introverted nature makes it difficult for him to openly challenge organizational expectations, especially when they clash with local needs or seasonal realities. Instead, he carries this struggle quietly, sharing his frustrations only with a few trusted colleagues. His sense of responsibility runs deep, but he often processes his challenges inwardly rather than outwardly advocating for change. Despite the obstacles, his quiet strength and dedication to serving others remain unwavering, even when the path is difficult.

Development Worker Profile Four—Dinesh and Pooja, Young Evangelistic Couple

Dinesh and Pooja, both converts from different religious backgrounds, relocated to a new area when Dinesh secured employment there. Deeply committed to their faith, they began prayer-walking through local communities; they prayed quietly and shared the message of Christ with those who were open and interceded for healing and deliverance. Over time, they witnessed numerous instances where prayer led to physical and spiritual restoration among the people.

Within two years, they established three house churches among the Chamar and Mushar communities—some of the most marginalized populations, living in extreme poverty with limited access to education and basic services. Beyond evangelism and church planting, they began mobilizing resources from their personal networks to address urgent material needs within these communities. When a US-based Christian organization observed the fruit of their ministry, they began offering small-scale organized support. Recognizing the growing scope of their work, the couple sought to formalize their ministry by registering as a non-governmental organization. They desired to serve their communities in a more structured and sustainable way.

One of the couple's greatest strengths is their genuine commitment to building relationships within their community. They take time to listen to individuals, offering prayer and support with sincerity and empathy. This approach not only fosters trust but also strengthens their ministry as they work to establish house churches and nurture discipleship. Despite the challenges they face, they remain eager to learn new skills and continuously strive to organize their work more effectively. Their prayerful attitude reflects a deep reliance on God, as they intentionally seek to ensure that their primary trust remains in the Lord rather than external financial support from the USA. They remain committed to their vision of seeing house churches grow and multiply as disciples share Christ with others.

However, their path is not without significant challenges. One pressing issue is the bureaucratic delay in obtaining NGO registration approval from the government. Their application is stalled, requiring endorsements from multiple government agencies. Although a local lawyer is assisting them in navigating this complex process, progress remains slow. The temptation to expedite the process by offering bribes is real, as it could significantly speed up the approvals. Yet, their convictions against bribery keep them resolute in maintaining integrity, even when faced with the frustration of stalled paperwork. They pray that the necessary approvals will come through without compromising their ethical standards. Amid these challenges, they remain focused on their mission and determined not to lose sight of their vision for the community.

Development Worker Profile Five—Lamung, an Urban Pastor in a Conflict Zone

In a city deeply affected by ongoing conflict, Lamung chooses to remain with his people despite opportunities to emigrate. He was on the verge of leaving for the US, where his sister had sponsored him and his family to join her, but he felt the Lord calling him to remain among his community. He witnesses the arrival of thousands of internally displaced persons fleeing violence, and he leads his church to respond with practical compassion.

They initially offer vocational training in skills such as welding and carpentry to help displaced young people achieve self-sufficiency.

He recognizes the need for a broader, more coordinated response, and so he brings together a network of churches in the region. Some congregations donate land for housing construction, while others repurpose their church buildings as temporary schools during the week. As collaboration deepens, the network formalizes its efforts and establishes a more organized and strategic support system for displaced communities—rooted in the shared witness, generosity, and commitment of local churches. The pastor who initiates this movement continues to serve as the network's coordinator and facilitator.

The church network is firm in its commitment to support the displaced people who have recently arrived in their communities, despite the significant challenges involved. One of the uncertainties is whether these individuals will remain long-term or return to their original homes once the conflict subsides. Many fled hastily, leaving behind essential documents, and without identity papers, they face severe restrictions on movement and access to services. Helping these individuals obtain legal identification is a priority for church leaders, but it is particularly difficult for certain ethnic minorities to secure such papers from the government.

The pastors navigate this complex situation with caution, aware that their compassionate efforts could be misinterpreted by authorities as support for militia groups. This risk makes their work politically sensitive and requires them to exercise wisdom—being as "innocent as doves and sharp as serpents"—as they serve those in need. While they strive to help within their capacity, local resources are limited. To bridge the gap, they have sought assistance from a Christian organization based in the US. However, the challenges of obtaining a formal NGO registration in their conflict context complicates the process of receiving international funds, forcing them to rely on informal channels. Despite these obstacles, the pastors remain steadfast, balancing their commitment to the displaced with the need to maintain cautious relationships with government authorities. They demonstrate resilience and resourcefulness, guided by prayer and the conviction to act with both integrity and compassion.

EMPOWERED TO SERVE, CALLED TO DISCERN

To sum up, fieldworkers occupy a pivotal yet often underappreciated role in the practice of Transformational Development. The five profiles of development workers reflect the dynamic and challenging realities of transformational development, highlighting how fieldworkers exemplify transformational values while navigating the tension between relational engagement, program delivery, and community realities. Moses exemplifies resilience and deep calling. Despite organizational demands that sometimes undermine genuine transformation, he was driven by his faith to address community needs, and he demonstrated his dedication to holistic change. Similarly, Ruth balances community ownership with personal sacrifice and builds strong relationships while grappling with the pressure to shift from face-to-face engagement to technology-driven reporting in response to the need for greater efficiency. In contrast, Sokchean, with his creativity and quiet dedication, integrates agricultural skills with community-based development. He fosters trust through playful interactions, though his introverted nature makes it difficult to openly challenge organizational expectations. Dinesh and Pooja, committed to both relational ministry and practical support, embody integrity by resisting bureaucratic shortcuts. They demonstrate their commitment to resolving the hurdles of formal registration. Meanwhile, Lamung's adaptive leadership shines as he remains rooted among his community despite opportunities to leave, fostering collaboration while cautiously navigating political sensitivities. Together, these profiles illustrate how transformational development requires to manage tensions between organizational demands, program delivery, and the reality of grassroots ministry, with each worker demonstrating resilience, creativity, and faithfulness in the face of complex challenges.

Fieldworkers' agency is essential, not only for adaptive decision-making and contextual responsiveness but also for preserving the dignity and participation of those they serve. Yet, the very systems within which they work often constrain that agency and pull them between the relational demands of community work and the technical imperatives for organizational performance. Recognizing, supporting, and safeguarding fieldworkers' agency is not simply an operational concern; it is a theological, ethical, and strategic imperative for any organization committed to holistic and Christ-centered development. In the subsequent chapters, we will continue to address these tensions with honesty and intentionality as we seek to honor both the people in communities and those called to walk alongside them.

The call to walk with communities in their journey of transformation echoes the incarnational pattern of Jesus, who entered into the world not to control it from above, but to live among us, full of grace and truth (John 1:14). Fieldworkers, too, are called to a ministry of presence. They do not simply deliver solutions, but they listen, learn, and love in ways that reflect Christ's humility and compassion. As Paul reminds readers in 2 Cor 5:20, "We are therefore Christ's ambassadors, as though God were making his appeal through us." The role of ambassador is not one of domination, but of reconciliation—inviting people into wholeness while walking humbly beside them. When fieldworkers are given the space to exercise their God-given agency, they reflect the image of a God who empowers rather than overrides, and who calls rather than coerces.

2

Theories of Development and the Role of Fieldworkers

Why Theories Matter

In the previous chapter, we explored who fieldworkers are, why their agency matters, and the unique tensions they experience as they serve at the interface between communities and the Christian organizations they represent. These dynamics do not occur in a vacuum. Not all Christian organizations engaged in holistic ministry understand or approach Transformational Development (TD) in the same way. While they may share core convictions, they often differ in how they define problems, envision solutions, and determine their role in addressing them. These differences are shaped by what we call a *theory of change*.

A Christian organization's understanding, articulation, and practice of TD profoundly influences the role of fieldworkers. This influence stems from the organization's underlying development frameworks, often referred to as theories of change, which organizations sometimes explicitly state, often implicitly assume, and define how they identify problems, envision solutions, design programs, allocate resources, and evaluate outcomes. Critically, the theory of change an organization adopts also shapes the day-to-day realities of fieldworkers: the extent of their agency, the degree of decision-making freedom they exercise, and how they are perceived by the communities they serve. This chapter examines some of the major development theories that inform TD in practice, with particular attention to their implications for fieldworkers.

UNDERSTANDING THEORIES OF CHANGE IN PRACTICE

Most organizations that seek to bring about transformational changes, whether at the community, national, or global level, hold an implicit or explicit theory of how change happens. These theories articulate an organization's assumptions about the current state of the world, the root causes of the problems they seek to address, the actors and systems involved, and the organization's own unique contribution to the desired future. In some organizations, the theory of change is formalized as an official policy or shared publicly. In others, it remains unwritten; staff and leadership hold it in the collective memory or tacitly assume it in how they do strategies and plans. Regardless of formality or complexity, these theories guide decisions about what to do, how to do it, and what success looks like. Larger global organizations tend to hold more complex theories of change, while smaller, local organizations may operate with simpler frameworks aligned with specific goals. Importantly, no organization operates in a vacuum. Multiple influences, organizational culture, leadership worldviews, donor requirements, and practical experiences all shape theories of change. In some cases, different or even contradictory theories coexist within a single organization. Fieldworkers, positioned at the intersection of these dynamics, must interpret and enact these frameworks on the ground, and they often blend multiple logics into their daily work.

What is written in organizational theory of change documents does not always match how change unfolds in practice. A host of factors influence real world implementation—personal beliefs, organizational culture, resource limitations, and managerial systems, among others. Donors may bring their own theories of change, which may or may not align with the implementing organization's view. This disconnect often leads to blended or conflicted frameworks, which create ambiguity at the field level. Despite these complexities, theories of change deeply shape how organizations set priorities, and structure interventions. Since fieldworkers implement the interventions, these theoretical assumptions directly influence how they carry out their work, what is expected of them, and how they are empowered or constrained in their roles.

FOUR MAJOR THEORIES UNDERPINNING DEVELOPMENT

Although there is no single unified theory of change for Transformational Development, most organizational approaches can be grouped under four broad development paradigms, which I have adopted from Bob Mitchell, a Christian development theorist and author.[1] Each group of theories reflects distinct assumptions about how change occurs and what role fieldworkers play:

1. *Rationalist-Managerial Theories:* Development is seen as a technical process, best managed by experts. These theories emphasize planning, control, and measurable outputs; fieldworkers frequently implement predesigned interventions.

2. *Participatory-Learning Theories:* Development arises through the active participation and empowerment of communities. Change is relational and emergent; fieldworkers facilitate dialogue, learning, and locally defined action.

3. *Rights-Based and Justice-Oriented Theories:* Development is framed as a struggle for justice and equity. This group of theories focus on challenging structural inequalities and claiming rights. Fieldworkers mobilize and advocate to help communities engage with power structures.

4. *Complexity and Adaptive Systems Theories:* Development is understood as dynamic, nonlinear, and networked; it requires experimentation, iteration, and contextual adaptation. Fieldworkers innovate and make sense in an unpredictable environment.

Organizations rarely operate under a single paradigm. Most combine elements of multiple theories, though usually one is dominant. The prevailing theory can often be identified by examining key performance indicators, language in planning documents, and patterns of resource allocation. Other theories may be present, but only in service of the dominant logic. Each group of theories casts fieldworkers in a different light: whether as technicians, facilitators, advocates, or innovators. These roles are not neutral; they reflect deeper assumptions about who holds knowledge, how power is distributed, and what constitutes meaningful change. In the sections that

---

1. Mitchell, *Faith-Based Development*, 34.

follow, we will explore each of these groups of theories in greater depth and highlight their assumptions about poverty, their implications for TD, and their practical consequences for fieldworkers. The table below compares four groups of development theories based on their assumptions, areas of focus, the role of fieldworkers, and the implications for fieldworker agency.

Table 2.1: Fieldworker Roles Across Development Paradigms: A Comparative Overview

Development Theories	Core Assumptions	Primary Focus	Role of Fieldworker	Implications for Agency
Rationalist, Managerial	Change is achieved through technical planning and expert-led interventions	Technical soundness, measurement of outputs and outcomes	Faithful implementer, Technician	Limited: Follow prescribed plans and deliverables
Participatory, Learning	Change arises from collective reflection and action by community members	Empowerment and local ownership	Facilitator of dialogue, participatory processes, and co-learning	Moderate to high, supports local decision-making
Rights-Based, Justice-Oriented	Change results from addressing structural injustices and claiming entitlements	Advocacy, justice and equity	Mobilizer, Advocate, or Activist	High, often acts politically and challenges structures
Complex Adaptive Systems	Change is emergent, nonlinear, shaped by learning within complex environments	Innovation, networking, and contextual adaptation	Sense-maker, innovator, and adaptive navigator	High, empowered to respond flexibly and experiment

RATIONALIST, MANAGERIAL APPROACHES TO DEVELOPMENT

Rationalistic approaches to development are grounded in the assumption that well-defined cause and effect relationships can be employed to bring about measurable improvements in people's lives. These approaches prioritize evidence-based, data-driven interventions designed to produce predetermined results, especially in sectors such as health, education, agriculture, food security, and infrastructure. Scientific and technological advancements have played a vital role in improving the quality of life for people everywhere. For instance, the Green Revolution significantly increased food production in Asia. Vaccination campaigns have drastically reduced childhood diseases like polio, measles, and tetanus. In recent years, mobile banking platforms like M-Pesa in Kenya and renewable energy technologies such as solar power have expanded access to essential services. Innovations in agriculture, digital health, education, and disaster response all underscore how science and technology, built on cause-and-effect logic, can drive development. At the heart of this approach is the belief that interventions, when applied consistently, will produce predictable outcomes, regardless of location. Whether it is delivering vaccines, purifying water, or applying fertilizer, rationalistic development assumes replicability of results as long as technical standards are met.

Cause-and-Effect Logic in Practice

The rationalistic model relies on relationships between independent variables (causes) and dependent variables (effects). These relationships are often established through controlled experiments and empirical research. For example, a child receiving a measles vaccine develops immunity to the virus—an observable and measurable effect from a specific input. Similarly, applying fertilizer at the right time leads to increased crop yield. These examples highlight the strengths of rationalistic approaches when applied to areas with relatively stable and universal inputs, such as biological or environmental systems, where the outcomes can be measured objectively.

Where Rationalism Falls Short

While rationalistic approaches succeed in the physical sciences, their limitations become apparent when applied to social systems and complex change processes. Social behaviors, values, relationships, and power dynamics are not easily reducible to standardized inputs and outputs. For example, improving child nutrition may depend as much on intra-household dynamics and gender norms as it does on providing micronutrient supplements and a healthy diet. Similarly, addressing corruption, domestic violence, or conflict requires more than standardized solutions imported from other contexts. These problems demand relational, contextual, and adaptive responses—areas where a strict cause-effect logic falls short. With regard to these problems, development interventions must account for the complexity and unpredictability of human behavior, culture, and spiritual beliefs. Indeed, Myers reminds us that while science and technology are gifts from God that contribute to well-being, they must be seen as part of a larger picture. Technological solutions alone do not encompass the full scope of transformational development, especially when spiritual, relational, or systemic factors are at play.[2]

The Challenge of Context

An important criticism of rationalistic approaches is their tendency to prioritize what is globally acceptable over what is contextually appropriate. Technical specialists in development organizations often design interventions centrally in NGO headquarters and assume that technical solutions can be implemented uniformly across diverse settings, and contextual variations are understood as issues that can be managed at the time of implementation. However, local contexts vary in terms of social norms, religious beliefs, capacities, resources, and a range of other factors that require consideration right from the beginning. For example, a standardized literacy intervention that improves learning outcomes in one context may prove less effective in another, where differences in language use at home, parental literacy, school infrastructure, or cultural expectations around gender and education influence how children learn and whether families engage with the program. By imposing external solutions, programs that fail to adapt to local realities risk not only poor outcomes but also the alienation of the very people they aim to serve. People in traditional communities may not interpret problems through a scientific lens. As Myers notes, community members may attribute their suffering to spiritual realms rather than to naturalistic or material causes. While implementing programs based on the rationalistic model, fieldworkers must engage with these perspectives respectfully and not dismiss them as irrational or backward.[3]

---

2. Myers, *Walking with the Poor*, 237.
3. Myers, *Walking with the Poor*, 209.

A Biblical Perspective

From a Christian perspective, rationalism as a method can be a useful tool, but it should not be elevated to an all-encompassing worldview. God is the ultimate source of wisdom and every good gift (Jas 1:17). Scientific insight, technological advancement, and empirical reasoning are manifestations of God's common grace and reflect the human capacity for observation and creativity granted in the imago Dei (Gen 1:27–28). As such, the fruits of discovery, such as medical breakthroughs or agricultural improvements, should be received with gratitude and applied with humility. We see biblical examples of God working through rational, orderly processes: Noah was given detailed instructions for building the ark (Gen 6:14–16), and Joseph's food storage plan during the famine in Egypt reflects careful planning, logistics, and foresight (Gen 41:33–36). The book of Proverbs is filled with counsel on the value of prudence, discipline, and wise planning (Prov 21:5, 24:3–4), and Jesus himself noted the wisdom of counting the cost before building a tower (Luke 14:28–30). These passages affirm that thoughtful, strategic work has biblical precedent.

However, Scripture also makes clear that human life cannot be reduced to technical problem solving. True transformation involves spiritual and relational outcomes. Jesus did not heal or feed crowds merely to solve problems, but as signs to point people to God's kingdom in their midst. He restored dignity, offered forgiveness, and drew people into communion with God and one another (Mark 5:34 and John 6:35–40). People are not projects: they are image-bearers of God whose healing includes restored identity, community, and vocation. Rationalist approaches may offer helpful tools, but they must be located within the broader framework of God's redemptive mission to reconcile all things to himself (Col 1:19–20).

Conclusion: Value with Caution

Rationalistic approaches to development offer significant value, particularly in designing and implementing interventions that require technical soundness and managerial rigor. They have enabled life-saving innovations and increased access to essential services for millions. Yet we must acknowledge their limitations. These approaches can struggle to account for the complexity of human behavior, spiritual realities, and sociocultural contexts. They may unintentionally marginalize local knowledge, traditional wisdom, and the agency of communities and fieldworkers. For Christian organizations engaged in Transformational Development, the key is to integrate the strengths of rationalistic approaches within a broader framework that respects human dignity, promotes relational transformation, and aligns with God's purposes. Rationalism has its place, but it must be held within a broader understanding of how transformational changes happen.

PARTICIPATORY APPROACHES TO DEVELOPMENT

Participatory development emphasizes that people must be actively involved in shaping the changes that affect their lives. In this view, a development effort's effectiveness and sustainability hinge on whether people have a sense of ownership and agency. As Amartya Sen has pointed out, development cannot simply be about delivering well-being to people; it must uphold and enhance their ability to make choices and act on their own behalf.[4] Likewise, Myers asserts that if poverty reflects a marred sense of identity, then any transformation must include processes that restore agency and dignity through participation.[5] This emphasis on local ownership echoes well with the democratic values of many donor agencies and the faith commitments of Christian development organizations. As Alan Fowler noted, there is compelling evidence that development outcomes are more sustainable when communities themselves help define and co-own the change process.[6]

Critiques of Participation

Despite widespread support for participation, participatory discourse has not been free of criticism. Scholars like Bill Cooke and Uma Kothari have pointed out that participation can become a tool for legitimizing external agendas rather than a genuine effort to empower communities.[7] Participatory tools, such as timelines, mapping exercises, or ranking matrices, can sometimes mask deeper power imbalances or serve an organization's bureaucratic requirements rather than people's aspirations.

4. Sen, *Development as Freedom*, 190.
5. Myers, *Walking with the Poor*, 214.
6. Fowler, *Virtuous Spiral*, 22–22.
7. Cooke and Kothari, *Participation*, 14.

In such cases, participation becomes instrumental: a means to project legitimacy and achieve predetermined objectives, rather than an end in itself. Robert Chambers, one of the most prominent advocates of participatory approaches, recognizes this danger. He warns that professionals often bring biases rooted in specialization, reductionism, and a desire for standardization. These are biases that can distort their engagement with the lived realities of poor communities.[8] While participatory tools like Participatory Rural Appraisal (PRA) and Participatory Learning and Action (PLA) were developed to shift power back to local people, they can be misused if applied without humility or critical reflection.

Fieldworkers as Facilitators of Empowerment

In a participatory approach, fieldworkers are not seen as service providers or technical experts implementing a plan but as facilitators who help communities to reflect, decide, and act. This development approach provides the basis for empowerment, the process through which people become critically aware of their situations, recognize their God-given agency, and take action. Empowerment involves more than providing access to resources; it includes facilitating/working toward shifts in identity, confidence, and relationships, especially for those who are marginalized or excluded, and it aligns with Paulo Freire's understanding of humanization and liberation.[9] As Chambers puts it, fieldworkers must undergo a "reversal of roles." Those who are considered "uppers," technically trained, organizationally empowered staff, must intentionally disempower themselves to make space for others to lead. This means shifting from being controllers to coaches, and from instructors to listeners.[10]

From a Christian perspective, this reversal of roles aligns with the model of power and service that Jesus demonstrated. Jayakumar Christian calls this the power of powerlessness—choosing to serve and elevate others rather than dominate.[11] David J. Bosch similarly reminds us that Christian mission is rooted not in certainty and power but in vulnerability and weakness, as symbolized by the cross.[12]

8. Chambers, *Whose Reality Counts?*, 32.
9. Freire, *Pedagogy of the Oppressed*, 44.
10. Chambers, *Whose Reality Counts?*, 235–36.
11. Christian, *God of Empty-Handed*, 182–90.
12. Bosch, *Transforming Mission*, 515.

Bottom-Up Planning and the Challenge of Institutional Expectations

Truly participatory planning requires that communities, not just professionals, define problems, set priorities, and design actions. The role of the fieldworker is to enable these processes with humility and integrity. However, participatory rhetoric can be difficult to align with institutional realities. Fieldworkers are typically accountable to achieve the organization's program targets, timelines, and donor expectations. This dual accountability can create significant tension: on one hand, fieldworkers aim to empower communities to define their own path; on the other hand, organizations expect compliance with pre-defined plans. This tension increases when participatory methodologies are used performatively to produce visible outputs like community maps or planning charts that satisfy organizational evaluations but do not deepen community ownership. David Mosse cautions that such tools can become representative artifacts rather than instruments of transformation.[13] True participation requires that organizations empower their own staff, especially fieldworkers, by giving them space for decision making, valuing their insights, and allowing time for relationship-building and reflection. Participation must begin within the organization before it can be expected in communities.

Including the Marginalized

Participatory approaches emphasize that the marginalized, those typically excluded from community decision-making processes due to gender, caste, ethnicity, disability, or age, are intentionally included. Without this, participatory processes risk reinforcing existing hierarchies rather than challenging them. Fieldworkers are therefore are required to actively identify and engage those people who are often invisible in community meetings or overlooked in planning processes. They must also be alert to how dominant community groups may co-opt participatory processes to serve their own interests. True participation does not seek a consensus that masks inequity but facilitates the difficult conversations that expose and address structural injustices.

Fieldworkers orient and enable a community to pay sufficient attention to the structural differentiation that exists within a community

---

13. Mosse, *Cultivating Development*, 94.

such as differences in gender, ethnicity, caste, and other contextual variables. The Jamkhed Comprehensive Rural Health Project demonstrates this process; it was founded in 1970 in Maharashtra, Central India by Rajanikant and Mabelle Arole, who were motivated by their Christian faith. Their innovative approach influenced the 1978 Alma-Ata Declaration of World Health Organization. They empowered illiterate women, primarily widows and outcasts, to provide health education, improve child feeding practices, and offer basic healthcare. The Aroles also empowered outcasts and marginalized individuals to become change agents whom others had to approach for essential medical care. These individuals also played central roles in initiatives such as installing hand pumps, harvesting rainwater, teaching adult literacy classes, and promoting hygiene. In time, they became vital interlocutors within their communities. Such activities turned marginalized people from project beneficiaries to empowered change agents in their own communities. The project showcased the effectiveness of illiterate female Community Health Workers in providing basic health education, preventive care, and supportive services, bridging the gap between health systems and people they serve. In 1970, the region faced dire health and poverty challenges that included high infant mortality, malnutrition, and low healthcare access. However, within five years, infant mortality dropped, antenatal care and safe deliveries rose significantly, immunization rates soared, and leprosy cases reduced by half. By 1990, infant mortality was just twenty-six per thousand live births, family planning improved, malnutrition decreased, and tuberculosis cases reduced significantly. Today, all pregnant women receive antenatal care, childhood malnutrition is rare, and infant mortality is only fifteen deaths per thousand live births. This represents a remarkable achievement compared to similar rural populations in Maharashtra.[14]

Local Knowledge and Shared Learning

Finally, participatory development is built on the premise that local people possess knowledge that is essential to any development effort's success. Affirming local knowledge does not mean sentimentalizing indigenous knowledge or rejecting technical expertise. Rather, it calls for a fusion of horizons, where technical knowledge and local experience are brought into dialogue. Program approaches like Positive Deviance/Hearth to address

14. Perry and Rohde, "Jamkhed and Alma-Alta," 704.

moderate malnutrition among children under five years of age embody this integration well. Fieldworkers identify local families who succeed in keeping their children well-nourished despite facing the same challenges as other community members; then they spread these community-generated practices more widely. This strategy identifies solutions that emerged from within the community rather than being imposed from outside. Even so, fieldworkers must remain critically engaged: not all local practices are benign. Harmful traditions, such as child marriage or female genital mutilation, must be addressed sensitively and respectfully through listening and dialogue, as grounded in long-term relationships. As one fieldworker in India described, transformation often begins not with a program, but with time, prayer, and persistent presence.

Biblical Perspectives on Participatory Development

The Bible provides strong theological grounding for participatory approaches by affirming the dignity, agency, and relational nature of all people. Rooted in the creation narrative, all human beings are made in the image of God, which bestows on them intrinsic worth and a capacity for meaningful agency (Gen 1:26–27). Poverty, education, and social status do not limit this divine image-bearing; development must be done with people and not for them. Jesus' ministry models radical inclusion and participation. He invited ordinary people, fishermen, tax collectors, women, and the poor, not only to follow him but to become partners in his mission (Luke 10:1–3 and John 15:15). His use of parables and open dialogue as well as his responsiveness to questions illustrate a relational and participatory style of engagement. Similarly, the Apostle Paul presents the church as the body of Christ, wherein each member is essential and interdependent (1 Cor 12:12–27). This image affirms a participatory ethic where all contributions are honored, especially those from "weaker" or marginalized members.

However, participation is not always virtuous or redemptive. Scripture warns us in Exod 23:2 against uncritical group consensus. "Do not follow the crowd in doing wrong," God commands, reminding us that the majority is not always right. The biblical narrative repeatedly shows that God often works through the courageous obedience of individuals (e.g., Noah, Moses, Esther, Daniel, and the prophets), who stood alone against dominant cultural norms. Elijah believed he was the only one left faithful, yet God honored his solitary stand for truth (1 Kgs 19:10). The crowd that shouted "Hosanna!" soon cried out, "Crucify him!" Manipulated by religious leaders, they were caught in a tide of collective injustice. These stories highlight a critical tension: participation must be weighed against truth, justice, and righteousness. Group processes can easily be co-opted by the powerful or manipulated to reinforce harmful norms. Therefore, participatory development must be guided by biblical principles including justice for the vulnerable, truth-telling, prophetic challenge, and accountability before God.

Moreover, in the kingdom of God, participation is not an end in itself but a means of discernment and obedience. The goal is not to affirm all perspectives equally but to cultivate a community where God's voice is discerned in and through the people, particularly the poor and the marginalized, whose voices are too often silenced. Participation in development aligns with the biblical call to servant leadership (Mark 10:42–45), mutual submission (Eph 5:21), and community-building rooted in humility and love. Yet it must always be evaluated through the lens of God's justice and truth. Not all participation is holy, and not all consensus leads to flourishing. Participatory approaches, when shaped by the values of the kingdom, can reflect the heart of God. They must also remain open to prophetic correction and the uncomfortable work of confronting injustice, even within the community itself.

RIGHTS-BASED APPROACHES TO DEVELOPMENT

Rights-based approaches to development are grounded in the belief that all people, by virtue of being humans and citizenship, possess inherent rights that entitle them to basic services and protections. These rights are defined by universal human rights frameworks and written in national laws and policies. In this model, development is not merely about service delivery or improving livelihoods through projects; rather, it is about mobilizing citizens to understand, claim, and exercise their rights, in order to hold duty-bearers, typically government entities, accountable for upholding those rights. This approach views individuals not as passive recipients of aid or participants in externally funded initiatives but as active claim-making agents and citizens who are entitled to engage in civic life and to influence how services are designed, delivered, and evaluated.[15] Development, thus, becomes a matter of participatory citizenship, especially for those who have

---

15. Hickey and Mohan, *From Tyranny to Transformation*, 3.

been historically excluded. Equitable and lasting change necessitates their inclusion in decision-making and governance processes. Rights-based development emphasizes two primary avenues for civic participation:

1. Claiming specific entitlements and services, such as education, healthcare, and protection, by demanding accountability and transparency from government service providers.
2. Forming associations or community-based groups that counter poor governance, engage in social audits, and advocate for improved public services through collective voice and action.[16]

Several tools and methods are commonly employed as part of this approach, including citizen report cards, participatory budgeting, social audits, and Citizen Voice and Action (CVA), a notable example from practice that is often facilitated by fieldworkers who build trust and guide the process and ensure community voices are heard and acted upon. CVA strengthens accountability between citizens and government service providers through collaborative, non-confrontational processes. CVA typically unfolds in three phases:

1. *Public Awareness*: Fieldworkers educate citizens about the government's policies, service standards, and entitlements (e.g., for primary education, citizens would learn provisions for access, and requirements for teaching quality, school facilities, etc.).
2. *Community Monitoring and Scoring*: Citizens use participatory tools to compare actual services against established standards to assess the quality of services they receive.
3. *Interface and Joint Action Planning*: Service users, providers, and local government officials engage in dialogue facilitated by fieldworkers and agree on specific actions and individuals to improve services.

In this paradigm, fieldworkers act as facilitators and educators. Their role includes building community awareness of civic rights, organizing participatory forums, and strengthening relationships between communities and state actors. They help ensure that local citizens are informed and empowered to advocate for their rights and engage constructively with government service providers.

---

16. Mohanty and Tandon, *Participatory Citizenship*, 13.

Critiques of Rights-Based Approaches

While rights-based approaches offer a compelling framework for justice and accountability, they are not without significant challenges and limitations, especially when implemented by external NGOs. These challenges are explained below.

Mandate and legitimacy: A key concern is when the rights-based approach becomes a self-assumed mandate of the NGO or INGO. Unlike people's organizations or grassroots-based movements, most external development organizations derive neither their legitimacy nor operational mandates from the communities they serve. They often operate as charitable entities funded by donors from other countries. This dynamic raises ethical questions about whether such organizations should facilitate local citizens' efforts to hold their governments accountable, especially when those same organizations are not fully accountable to those communities themselves.[17]

Effectiveness in weak states: Rights-based strategies depend on the presence of a functioning state capable of providing basic services and engaging with citizens. However, in many low-income contexts, the state is either too weak, under-resourced, corrupt, or unresponsive. The *Voices of the Poor* study highlights how many poor people perceive the state as ineffective or even hostile; they describe interactions with state representatives as humiliating, corrupt, or obstructive.[18] In such contexts, rights-based efforts risk becoming symbolic or even disempowering if citizens' claims are routinely ignored.

Elite capture and unequal benefits: Studies also reveal that decentralization and participatory governance initiatives can be co-opted by local elites. Rather than promoting equity, these approaches may reproduce existing power hierarchies. For instance, when governance is decentralized, local elites often gain disproportionate control and steer benefits toward their networks while excluding the most vulnerable.[19]

Population level benefits over marginalized communities: Rights-based frameworks are often more effective at promoting universal benefits (such as education or disease control) that serve both the poor and the non-poor. However, they are less effective in targeting highly marginalized groups, particularly when their needs conflict with the interests of the broader or

---

17. Bornstein, *Spirit of Development*, 102.
18. Narayan-Parker et al., *Voices of the Poor*, 5.
19. Blair, "Participation and Accountability," 25.

dominant community. For example, while a CVA process might successfully improve education services across a district, it may not address the specific water access needs of a socially ostracized group within a single village.

Preconditions for success: Rights-based approaches work best when there are functioning government systems, space for citizens to participate, and active community groups. Without these conditions, efforts to promote citizen involvement are likely to fail.[20] Despite these criticisms of rights-based approaches, they do have strengths. Rights-based approaches can:

- Improve public service quality through increased accountability.
- Build civic capacity and confidence among local communities.
- Provide a non-confrontational framework for advocacy and citizen engagement.
- Foster collaborative problem-solving between citizens and state actors.

In this sense, even if such approaches fall short of delivering deep structural transformation or exclusive focus on the most vulnerable, they still offer meaningful improvements in governance, services, and civic voice, especially when fieldworkers serve as trusted facilitators who can build relationships and help community members navigate complex power dynamics.

Biblical Reflections on Rights-Based Approaches to Development

From a biblical perspective, the pursuit of justice is not simply a moral duty or a social good, it is a core attribute of God's character. Scripture repeatedly affirms that God is a God of justice who defends the cause of the vulnerable. The Old Testament law provided numerous protections for the widow, the orphan, the poor, and the foreigner (Deut 10:17–19 and Isa 1:17). These protections were not just optional acts of mercy, but they demonstrate a grounding in the understanding of covenantal obligations that reflect God's desire for just relationships within the community.

Rights-based approaches to development emphasize human dignity and people's entitlements, themes that resonate with the biblical truth that all human beings are created in the image of God and thus possess inherent worth (Gen 1:27–27). The prophetic tradition in Scripture often challenges

20. Gaventa and McGee, "Impact of Transparency," s12.

the abuse of power and exploitation by the wealthy or ruling classes (Amos 5:11–15). Jesus himself announced his mission mandate by quoting Isaiah; he proclaimed good news to the poor and freedom to the oppressed, and he framed his kingdom mission as deeply concerned with justice and restoration (Luke 4:18–19).

However, while the language of rights coheres with biblical themes of justice, the biblical vision goes further by calling not only for the claiming of rights but also for the exercise of responsibility, mutual care, and stewardship. In the New Testament, Paul appeals not to rights alone, but to love, sacrifice, and servanthood (Phil 2:1–8 and 1 Cor 9:3–18). Thus, in Christian development practice, rights may be pursued: not in a confrontational manner that reinforces antagonism but in a spirit of humility, advocacy for marginalized people, and relational justice.

For fieldworkers, the biblical imperative is clear: advocate for the voiceless (Prov 31:8–9), walk humbly with God, act justly, do mercy, and engage in restorative practices that build dignity and trust. Fieldworkers' efforts to facilitate voice, promote accountability, and nurture responsible governance echo the kingdom values of justice, mercy, and reconciliation. Yet, it must be done with spiritual discernment, relational integrity, and a deep awareness of context.

DEVELOPMENT AS AN EMERGENT, ADAPTIVE SYSTEM

Emergent or adaptive approaches to development have gained traction in response to the reality that many development challenges are complex, dynamic, and deeply interconnected. Rather than treating development problems as technical puzzles with clear solutions, adaptive approaches frame them as complex systems that require iterative learning, experimentation, and responsiveness to context. Unlike traditional models that rely on fixed goals, linear planning, and standardized interventions, adaptive development embraces uncertainty, change, and learning. It is not primarily driven by rigid frameworks (e.g., logframes) or strictly predefined outcomes. Instead, it operates on the principle that plans are best used as a compass to offer direction, rather than as a map with predetermined routes. Key elements include flexibility, local ownership, network-based innovation, and the ability to pivot strategies as new insights emerge.

In their respective works, Duncan Green, Ben Ramalingam, and David Peter Stroh, each of whom are development scholars and practitioners, emphasize the importance of recognizing the dynamic and context-specific nature of development work. Green advocates for a "power and systems approach" that acknowledges the complexity of social change and the need for adaptive strategies.[21] Ramalingam critiques traditional linear models of aid, suggesting that development challenges are better addressed through complexity science and adaptive systems thinking.[22] Stroh underscores the necessity of understanding underlying structures and patterns to effectively tackle complex social issues.[23] Collectively, these authors argue for development practices that are responsive to the intricate and evolving contexts in which they operate. One simple example illustrates this well: an NGO working to combat childhood malnutrition initially employed a standardized approach, providing supplementary feeding and livelihood assistance, aligned with a predesigned logframe and a system for reporting on standard indicators. However, fieldworkers soon observed that persistent malnutrition resulting from food insecurity was rooted in deeper, localized structural issues. These included land tenure disputes with local temple trustees that prevented families from accessing adequate land for cultivation; water salinization caused by commercial shrimp farming, which led to poor crop yields; the presence of liquor shops contributing to alcoholism, which in turn reduced household spending on nutritious food; and systemic corruption within public services. While technical nutrition interventions were important, they alone could not resolve the problem of malnutrition on a sustainable basis. The field staff believed that addressing malnutrition required integrated, holistic action rooted in the realities of local communities. But organizational rigidity and a reductionist program model, focused solely on nutritional interventions and metrics, prevented flexibility. In this case, the development challenge was not just malnutrition, but the organization's inability to adapt its approach to adaptive challenges in different communities.

Critiques and Limitations

While adaptive development approaches have become more popular in development discourse, their practical implementation remains uncertain. One key critique is that the concept of adaptive development

---

21. Green, *How Change Happens*, 235–57.
22. Ramalingam, *Aid on the Edge of Chaos*, 135–40.
23. Stroh, *Systems Thinking*, loc. 388–486.

often lacks clarity. There is little consensus on what "adaptive" actually means in practice and how it should be operationalized. Another concern is for the gap between rhetoric and reality. Many organizations claim to adopt adaptive approaches, but they remain constrained by funding cycles, performance metrics, and management systems that prioritize predictability, accountability, and scalability over experimentation and local adaptation. Donors and large NGOs often still demand clear outputs, measurable outcomes, and standardized indicators, which limit the space for adaptation.

Furthermore, adaptive development requires a significant shift in organizational culture. Hierarchical, risk-averse structures, which are common in many development agencies, can stifle innovation and learning. Real adaptation demands tolerance for ambiguity, willingness to accept failure as a learning process, and decentralization of decision-making authority. None of these traits are easily achieved.

Finally, the flexibility and learning central to adaptive approaches can lead to questions about accountability: if plans and goals keep changing, how can success be measured? How do organizations ensure that changes reflect community voices and do not merely shift donor agendas or managerial preferences?

Implications for Fieldworkers

For fieldworkers, adaptive development presents both opportunities and challenges. On one hand, it affirms their central role as observers, connectors, facilitators, and agents of learning and innovation. This approach values fieldworkers' proximity to the community, their contextual knowledge, and their ability to navigate dynamic, complex realities. Fieldworkers in adaptive systems do not merely implement predefined activities. They act as searchers, relationship builders, knowledge brokers, and boundary spanners. A boundary spanner is someone who connects people, groups, or organizations that usually operate separately, helping them share information, build trust, and work together more effectively.[24] Their job involves listening, learning, attempting small-scale interventions, reflecting on what does and does not work, and adjusting strategies in collaboration with communities and colleagues.

24. Williams, "Competent Boundary Spanner," 103–24.

However, for fieldworkers to express effectively these roles, they must be given freedom to experiment, make decisions, and take risks. This latitude requires a significant shift in how organizations manage and support their frontline staff. Fieldworkers must be empowered not only to learn but also to shape programs in response to that learning. They also need the time and space to build trust with communities, a task that cannot be easily rushed or fit into rigid logframes. In the example of the malnutrition program mentioned earlier, fieldworkers intuitively understood the systemic drivers of malnutrition. But their ability to act was curtailed by organizational structures that valued standardized delivery over contextual responsiveness. For adaptive development to succeed, such constraints must be removed.

Biblical Perspectives

Scripture deeply resonates with the ethos of adaptive development. Biblical narratives consistently reveal a God who works dynamically, who is sovereign over changing contexts, and who invites people into a journey of discernment and obedience. Throughout Scripture, God's sovereignty is held in perfect tension with human agency; each plays a vital role in advancing God's ultimate purposes. For example, God's dealings with Israel were not driven by rigid plans but by a covenantal relationship that unfolded over time. God gave Israelites many opportunities for learning, repentance, and transformation. Jesus' ministry was similarly adaptive. He responded to people's needs as they arose by healing, feeding, challenging, and teaching. Jesus often subverted expectations and offered new paths forward. The Spirit's role in guiding believers into truth underscores that truth unfolds and must be discerned over time, in community (John 16:13).

The emergence and spread of the early church as recorded in the book of Acts offers a compelling biblical example of a complex adaptive system in action. Jesus did not give the disciples a detailed strategic blueprint to fulfill the command of Acts 1:8, to be his witnesses in Jerusalem, Judea, Samaria, and to the ends of the earth. After Jesus ascended, they responded by waiting in obedience for the promised Holy Spirit. What followed was not a centralized, pre-planned expansion but a Spirit-led movement that grew through responsive leadership, local engagement, and divine guidance amid unfolding events. Peter's sermon at Pentecost, prompted by public questions and spiritual curiosity, marked the church's spontaneous birth in

Jerusalem. Later, acts of healing, persecution, and cross-cultural encounters led the church beyond Jerusalem—not through deliberate planning but through faithful responses to emerging opportunities and challenges.

As persecution scattered the believers, the gospel naturally extended to new regions and peoples. The apostles adapted. They affirmed and strengthened new communities, as seen in their response to the growing church in Samaria and the Gentile believers in Antioch. Leadership was not about controlling outcomes; they discerned and responded with wisdom to what the Spirit was doing. When cultural tensions arose between Jewish and Gentile believers, the leaders gathered, listened, and discerned a path forward; they demonstrated humility, contextual sensitivity, and spiritual discernment (Acts 15). This early church movement illustrates several principles relevant to Christian development in complex systems: faithful presence precedes strategic control; leadership must remain adaptive and responsive rather than directive; and the Spirit's leading, not human planning, determines the pace and direction of transformational change. These dynamics mirror the nature of transformational development—emerging, relational, Spirit-led, and grounded in trust, discernment, and responsive action.

Fieldworkers often serve in unpredictable and dynamic environments where detailed strategies can become obsolete. Their role is less about implementing rigid plans and more about cultivating presence, attentiveness, and faithful responsiveness to what God is already doing in the community. Fieldworkers need to remain spiritually grounded, relationally engaged, and able to adapt to evolving circumstances while holding fast to the mission. They express their leadership not in controlling situations but in wise facilitation. They work to strengthen local believers, affirm community agency, and navigate complexities with openness, humility, and grace. In this way, fieldworkers function as stewards within complex adaptive systems; they discern patterns, respond to emerging opportunities, and embody the hope of Christ in word and deed.

BRIDGING THEORIES AND FIELDWORKERS

In this chapter, we examined four major approaches to transformational development—rationalistic, participatory, rights-based, and adaptive. Each approach carries with it distinct assumptions about how change occurs, what roles communities and organizations play, and how success is defined and measured. These frameworks influence everything from strategic planning to field-level implementation. While they offer useful lenses, they also bring certain limitations. Rarely does an organization adopt one approach in isolation. In practice, these frameworks often co-exist, sometimes intentionally, and sometimes in tension.

The work of development does not happen in theory, it happens in context. And the fieldworker sits at the critical intersection between theory and lived experience. Regardless of which theory or theories of change an organization adopts, it is ultimately the fieldworker who embodies that theory in action. As Christian organizations seek to reflect biblical values of justice, love, humility, and transformation, the fieldworker positioning becomes especially crucial. Fieldworkers are not simply implementers of programs. They are the facilitators, translators, cultural navigators, advocates, and sometimes even quiet prophets, who help communities reimagine their circumstances through a lens of hope and dignity.

Weaving a Beautiful Mat

A useful metaphor for integrating these theories is the image of weaving a mat, as illustrated in the diagram below. In many communities, traditional hand-woven mats or baskets are a familiar and meaningful part of daily life. They can also serve as a useful metaphor for understanding how different elements of community-based development must work together. The vertical strands of the basket represent the technical or "hardware" components of development—standardized, evidence-based interventions that can be replicated, measured, and reported. These are often best practices known to be effective. For instance, when establishing Early Childhood Development (ECD) Learning Centers, hardware elements might include constructing safe facilities, designing structured daily schedules, maintaining appropriate child-to-caregiver ratios, and planning nutritious meals. These interventions reflect the rationalist dimension of development practice. Technical specialists take the lead in planning or designing the hardware or technical components of a program.

In contrast, the horizontal strands symbolize the "software" of development—the contextual realities, cultural values, relational dynamics, and spiritual and social dimensions that shape human life. In the context of ECD, this might involve adopting community-centered planning approaches, incorporating local stories and songs into the curriculum, involving parents as volunteers or contributors to learning materials, integrating spiritual and moral education, and building trust through inclusive community events. These elements are equally vital across all sectors of development and reflect participatory, adaptive, and rights-based approaches. Together, the hardware and software elements, like the strands of a woven mat, form a strong, functional, and contextually grounded whole. Fieldworkers should take the lead in planning or designing these software, contextual components of a program. One without the other is incomplete. Too much focus on technical solutions may lead to sterile programs disconnected from reality. Too much emphasis on process without direction may lead to confusion and lack of progress. The challenge is not to choose one over the other but to weave them skillfully together, guided by local wisdom, organizational learning, and biblical convictions.

Diagram 2.1—Weaving Development

Every metaphor has its limitations. In practice, the balance between vertical and horizontal strands will vary based on program objectives. Some initiatives may require a greater emphasis on the "software" such as relational dynamics, community engagement, and adaptive learning, in programs aimed at addressing sensitive issues like preventing violence against children or promoting gender equity. Yet even these programs benefit from including tangible, technical activities that provide concrete platforms for engagement and transformation. Conversely, programs that focus heavily on the "hardware" side, such as immunization campaigns or maternal and child health interventions, invariably encounter "software" realities such as trust-building with communities, navigating cultural norms, and addressing local power dynamics. No matter the emphasis, skillfully weaving together both dimensions remains critical to promoting development that is both effective and transformative.

Positioning Fieldworkers: From Implementers to Integrators

Fieldworkers hold a central position in this weaving process. Their credibility within local communities, especially among the most vulnerable, allows them to develop the trust necessary for participatory processes. Their proximity to communities enables them to notice shifts in context and adapt accordingly. Their embeddedness in specific contexts allows them to surface issues of justice, exclusion, and power that may be invisible to higher-level planners and technical specialists.

For fieldworkers to function in this integrative role, organizations must empower them, by giving them freedom to adapt technical interventions to local contexts, time and space for relationship-building, tools for capturing community voices, and organizational cultures that value learning from the field. In turn, fieldworkers must be equipped not only with technical skills but also with theological grounding, emotional intelligence, political sensitivity, and a commitment to long-term engagement.

Case Studies: Integrating Development Theories in Practice

Two compelling examples from different cultural and geographical settings, Lamay in Peru mentioned in the introduction chapter and Jamkhed in India, referenced earlier in this chapter, highlight how diverse development theories can be integrated by fieldworkers and local actors. These cases demonstrate that the transformational impact of development does not emerge solely from adherence to any one theory but rather from thoughtful blending of multiple approaches, rooted in local realities, spiritual convictions, and long-term commitment.

In the Sacred Valley of Peru, the collaboration between World Vision and the local Richarry-Ayllu Association (RAA) unfolded as a powerful expression of Transformational Development. While the project focused on maternal and child health, associated with rationalistic approaches, the initiative was deeply participatory: it did not rely solely on technical solutions or top-down planning. Community volunteers served as health promoters and maternal advisors, drawing on the training they had received and training materials they had been provided with. They built trust-based relationships and facilitated localized learning and behavioral change. Participatory tools like community maps and development ladders helped translate complex data into collective action. The goals of improving child health were anchored in both measurable outcomes and relational transformation.

Similarly, in Jamkhed, India, the work of Raj and Mabelle Arole (described earlier in this chapter) embodied an integrated approach to development rooted in both rationalistic health strategies and participatory empowerment. The project's technical foundations—maternal health, immunization, and hygiene—were essential to its success, but the vehicle for delivery was a network of illiterate women, many of whom were widows and outcasts. These women became community health workers, who not only delivered care but also shifted social dynamics. By promoting local knowledge, practicing inclusion, and equipping the most marginalized to serve others, the Jamkhed model exemplifies a participatory ethos. The network of women moved from being seen as burdens to becoming respected agents of change in their communities.

Both programs also had elements of rights-based development woven into the fabric of practice. In Peru, citizens' collaboration with community assemblies and district officials reflected a recognition of their entitlements and responsibilities under national health policy frameworks. The project in Jamkhed advanced health rights long before the term became common in development discourse, and aligned its efforts with global movements such as the Alma-Ata Declaration, which emphasized health as a fundamental human right and promoted primary healthcare for all. In both instances, fieldworkers played a pivotal role in helping community members understand and engage with government standards and entitlements, thus promoting accountability and responsiveness.

Moreover, both projects displayed adaptive and emergent characteristics. Development was not pre-scripted. In Lamay, community members gradually assumed greater responsibility, even initiating ecotourism ventures after external funding ceased. They expressed local ownership, as well as their own learning and adaptation. In Jamkhed, the Aroles responded to local needs as they emerged. The couple tailored their interventions and modified their model based on ongoing reflection and community engagement. Rather than adhering to rigid plans, the project participants followed a compass more than a map. They were constantly navigating complexity through iteration and dialogue.

Together, these two cases show that Transformational Development flourishes when diverse approaches are joined in a coherent relationship through collaboration of leaders, technical specialists, and the agency of local actors. The health strategies may have drawn from rationalistic logic, but they contributed to community transformation because fieldworkers embodied participatory values, thoughtfully engaged power structures, promoted community rights, and continually adapted to local realities. It is this integrative practice, rooted in love, justice, and humility, that lies at the heart of enduring transformation.

Organizational Conditions for Integrative Practice

Fieldworkers' effectiveness is not merely a function of personal skills; it is shaped by the organizational conditions in which they work. Organizations that adopt rigid, top-down, logic-driven strategies may inadvertently stifle the creativity and contextual responsiveness required for effective fieldwork. Conversely, organizations that promote managerial flexibility, distributed decision-making, learning from failure, and dialogical reflection are more likely to produce development outcomes that are both effective and just. These goals require a rethinking of organizational design, away from control and standardization and toward alignment, accountability, and mutual trust. Organizations must also model internally the kind of participatory, rights-affirming, and adaptive values they promote externally.

For Christian organizations, the integration of these approaches is not simply a matter of effectiveness; it is a matter of faithfulness. The biblical narrative affirms that transformation happens in relationship, through mutuality, humility, and the movement of the Holy Spirit. Jesus' ministry model was profoundly participatory, relational, and adaptive. He affirmed the dignity of the marginalized, disrupted unjust systems, and operated not from control but from love. Fieldworkers who follow Christ's example engage with community members as co-participants in the process of transformation. They walk with people, listen deeply, confront injustice, and reflect the character of God in their work. Theories of change may guide strategic thinking, but Christ-shaped presence is what brings lasting transformation.

In summary, theories of development—rationalistic, participatory, rights-based, and adaptive—each offer insights and tools for practice. But none of them alone is sufficient. Transformational development becomes real in places where the best of these theories are woven together and embodied in the everyday practice of fieldworkers. When organizations embrace both the vertical and horizontal strands of the weaving—technical and relational, universal and contextual—development ceases to be just a project and becomes a dynamic and participatory journey of transformation.

3

Between Metrics and Mission
Organizational Strategy and Field Practice
—The Call to Spirit-Led Strategy

IN THE PREVIOUS CHAPTER, we examined dominant theories of development that shape the work of Christian organizations engaged in holistic ministry, along with the associated challenges, limitations, and implications for fieldworkers. In this chapter, we turn our attention to how these theories are translated into practice, specifically through the strategies and program design, monitoring, and evaluation—and how these, in turn, influence the role of fieldworkers.

Christian NGOs operate in a rapidly changing landscape where expectations for accountability, results, and scalability often mirror the logic of the corporate world. Christian NGOs often eagerly seek out people with corporate experience and hope that they can transfer their skills and replicate their success in the NGO context. Strategic planning, once a foreign concept in faith-based NGOs, is now widely accepted. Christian NGOs outline their goals, objectives, and actions to achieve their vision within a specific time frame, typically three to five years. Tools such as SWOT (Strengths, Weaknesses, Opportunities, and Threats) analysis, Logical Frameworks (logframes), and Key Performance Indicators (KPIs) are common. While these methods can bring clarity and focus, they do risk overshadowing the spiritual, relational, adaptive, and contextual nature of transformational development. This chapter seeks to hold strategy of an organization accountable to its mission. It argues that these strategic tools must be subordinated to the Christian organization's vision, mission, and calling to foster holistic, Christ-centered transformation through relationships, community empowerment, and faithful presence and witness.

Strategic planning is not inherently incompatible with Transformational Development. On the contrary, a well-discerned strategy can be an act of stewardship and bring alignment between vision, resources, and actions. However, when strategy becomes a technocratic exercise—detached from mission, theology, prayer, and local wisdom—it can easily drift into managerialism and be driven primarily by what seems achievable through calculation and control. Organizations may reduce strategic risk-taking to a compliance mechanism and focus more on avoiding mistakes rather than being shaped by spiritual discernment and reliance on God. This tension is evident in the increased use of planning tools that emphasize measurability over purpose. While metrics are necessary for accountability and decision-making, there is danger in assuming that what is measurable is all that matters. Christian NGOs must be especially wary of this temptation, for the gospel invites us into a story that values presence, grace, and transformation. None of these can be plotted easily on a performance dashboard. The trend toward professionalization has resulted in both gains and losses. On the one hand, Christian NGOs have become more competent, efficient, and credible in the eyes of donors and partners. On the other hand, professionalization may lead to a subtle shift in identity, from prophetic witness to project delivery, and from transformative accompaniment with poor people and donors to transactional service. Transformational mission can become depersonalized and divorced from specific contexts and dependence on Holy Spirit's guidance.

We begin by acknowledging the value of strategic clarity but also call for a recovery of what makes Christian development distinct: its alertness to the Spirit, its rootedness in relationships, and its theological imagination. Strategy should serve these commitments and not replace them. The following sections will explore the historical evolution of strategy in NGOs, assess prevailing frameworks such as "managing for results," and examine the implications for monitoring and evaluation in Christian organizations pursuing the mission of TD. I will argue for a holistic, Spirit-led, and context-responsive approach that centers on the role of fieldworkers, their relationships with the poor, and the agency of local communities. We begin by asking what strategies Christian NGOs use and why they use them, whom they serve, and how these strategies reflect or distort TD work. Here is a brief overview of different schools of strategy formulation.

APPROACHES TO STRATEGY

To understand how organizations develop and implement strategies, Henry Mintzberg et al. draw from extensive research in the business sector. Mintzberg identifies three broad approaches to strategy formation: prescriptive, descriptive, and configuration or transformational.[1] These categories offer a helpful framework for reflecting on how strategy work unfolds in Christian NGOs, particularly as these groups navigate the tensions between planning, adaptability, and mission-driven responsiveness.

Prescriptive approaches emphasize a rational, linear process, in which strategy precedes structure and implementation. Internal capacities are aligned with external opportunities, often through formal tools that include the SWOT analysis, objective setting, operational planning, budget allocation, and performance accountability systems. This model assumes that strategy can be designed through careful analysis after which it is rolled out in sequential steps. In this approach, getting the content of strategy "right" is vital. Even in organizations committed to participation and empowerment, the prescriptive model often dominates strategic planning exercises, particularly when conducted at higher levels of management and driven by external pressures. For example, many international Christian NGOs conduct strategic planning as a highly structured, board-driven process led by senior executives and technical planners and have limited engagement from staff at the community level.

By contrast, descriptive approaches focus less on idealized strategic content that works from the top down and more on how strategies actually evolve. Descriptive models highlight the role of visionary or entrepreneurial leadership, organizational learning, balancing power dynamics, negotiation, and responsiveness to changing contexts. Descriptive strategy works as an emergent process that is messy and adaptive. It is shaped by people within the organization as they respond to unfolding realities. This model resembles what often happens at a local level in Christian development organizations where plans evolve informally through relationships, learning, and local innovation.

---

1. Mintzberg et al., *Strategy Safari*, 5–7.

Configuration approaches recognize that no single strategy model fits all circumstances. Organizations move through different strategic modes depending on their life-cycle, context, leadership, and challenges. Periods of relative stability are punctuated by moments of transformational change, whether driven by crises, leadership transitions, shifts in external funding, or internal reorientation. In this view, organizations adopt various strategy configurations at different times; change occurs through a series of shifts rather than through a continuous process. Once formed, the resulting strategy tends to stabilize and direct the organization's activities, at least until the next significant shift is required.

The development sector increasingly recognizes that strategy must be adaptive and responsive, particularly given the complex and emergent nature of social and spiritual transformation. Nevertheless, many Christian NGOs still lean heavily on prescriptive approaches when it comes to formal organizational planning. Larger or more mature organizations frequently see planning as a high-level management function led by senior staff who work closely with the chief executive and the board. In such contexts, strategic planning focuses on demonstrating coherence, legitimacy, growth, and alignment with donor priorities to deliver results and demonstrate success. Senior staff tend to emphasize the production of clearly articulated goals, outcomes, and indicators that can be quantitatively measured, aggregated, and reported. These kinds of plans do not attend to complexity.

This does not mean that Christian NGOs operate exclusively through prescriptive models. Many faith-based organizations emerge in their early stages from the vision of charismatic founders who act intuitively and adaptively in response to emerging needs and opportunities. In these phases, strategy is fluid and relational. However, as organizations grow and formalize their operations, especially when they begin to receive significant donor funding, they tend to shift toward more structured management systems. Flexibility gradually narrows as the organization increasingly relies on tools, metrics, and strategic blueprints developed at the top. Configuration or transformational approaches to strategy typically happen when large-scale external disruptions compel organizations to rethink their structure, identity, and operations. For example, many Christian NGOs shifted to emergency relief after the 2004 tsunami, adopted digital platforms during COVID-19, and transformed their presence and operations in contexts that become politically sensitive. Even as I write this, the 2025 suspension of the operations of the United States Agency for International

Development (USAID) is similarly forcing NGOs to reconfigure their funding models and strategic priorities. These shifts are rarely incremental: they resemble what Mintzberg calls a "quantum leap" in strategy and a complete realignment in response to crisis that often leads to innovation and deeper mission alignment.[2]

Understanding the multiple modes through which organizations form and adapt strategy gives new appreciation to the complex realities fieldworkers face. While many Christian NGOs articulate a vision of transformational development, their processes for developing strategy, monitoring, and evaluation can be influenced by a prescriptive logic that emphasizes planning, upward accountability, and control. Even when strategy emerges through configurational or transformational shifts prompted by external events, its formulation still happens through centralized decision-making processes. However, when it comes to implementation, field staff frequently interpret and adapt strategies based on local realities, relational dynamics, and the demands of real-time problem-solving. At times, they creatively adapt and reinterpret formal plans; at other times, they feel constrained by rigid frameworks that leave little space for local discretion. This divergence between centrally formulated strategy and contextually adapted practice reflects the complexity of fieldwork in dynamic and relational environments.

STRATEGIC PLANNING AND ITS ROLE IN CHRISTIAN ORGANIZATIONS PURSUING TD

Strategic planning can be a gift when it aligns with mission. It offers clarity to everyone in the organization about its direction, provides coherence to organizational activities, and ensures stewardship in how resources are allocated. Within Christian NGOs involved in TD, strategy can be a means to live out the calling faithfully in a world of change and complex needs. Strategic planning emerged in many NGOs in the late twentieth century to respond to the growing demand for transparency and accountability. However, strategy is never neutral. It always reflects assumptions regarding change, power, time, and value. When these organizations adopt strategic tools without critically examining their underlying assumptions, they may unintentionally undermine the very transformation they seek. For instance, strategies that emphasize scalability may favor large scale interventions

---

2. Mintzberg et al., *Strategy Safari*, 309.

over small, deeply relational processes, which take longer to bear results. A strong emphasis on cost efficiency can often depersonalize development and reduce people to metrics and outcomes. When strategies are shaped entirely by comprehensive, rational planning, they leave little room for the unexpected, the relational, and what some might call the "God-space."

Transformational development seeks the restoration of relationships—with God, ourselves, others, and creation. Strategy when shaped by the mission of TD should be sufficiently flexible to accommodate the dynamic nature of various contexts, the complexity of people's lives, and the agency of community members. For example, a prescriptive strategic objective might state: "Reduce stunting among children under five years of age by 25 percent across all program areas within three years by implementing the integrated nutrition model: appropriate breast-feeding and complementary feeding, monthly growth monitoring, micronutrient supplements, and diarrhea prevention." While technically sound, such a directive assumes that a single solution—the integrated nutrition model—can be applied uniformly, and accomplish the intended results regardless of context. As it is written, the objective limits fieldworker flexibility, sidelines community agency, and fails to address deeper, localized causes of malnutrition. In contrast, a context-sensitive objective might read, "Enable communities to improve the well-being and nutrition of children under five years of age by addressing context-specific drivers of child malnutrition through locally adapted, integrated approaches." This approach honors local ownership and opens space for a more holistic response that can include context-specific issues alongside the relevant technical interventions mentioned earlier. In one setting, that might involve addressing issues related to alcoholism and domestic violence; in another context it could require securing land rights or repairing irrigation systems; and in yet another, fieldworkers might find that partnering with local faith-based organizations can revive traditional food systems. A flexible strategic approach aligns with the relational vision of transformational development by recognizing that people's lives are complex, contexts are dynamic, and solutions must be co-created rather than imposed.

A key distinction must be made between strategy as planning and strategy as posture. Strategic planning focuses on setting goals, aligning activities, and tracking progress. Strategic posture, however, reflects the organization's underlying orientation: responsiveness, humility, and openness to surprise. Strategic posture provides the guiding intent behind the strategy.³ Christian organizations should adopt a posture of discernment when designing and implementing plans for TD in real world contexts. Strategy, once initially formulated, should be held loosely to allow space for adaptation in response to emergent opportunities and challenges, while still moving in alignment with the organization's mission and the overall direction. Strategy formulation and its implementation should not be completely divorced from each other. In practical terms, this means involving diverse voices in the strategic process: not only senior leaders and donors but also field staff, local churches, and community members. This commitment to TD in strategy means organizations should ask not only "What should we do?" but "Who should we become?" and "How do we walk faithfully in this context?" It also means avoiding overly comprehensive strategies that attempt to anticipate every possible question and instead to leave room for flexibility and adaptation. Iterative feedback loops between strategy formulation and implementation make strategies more responsive to the lived realities of field staff in their daily work.

Any strategy for TD must be evaluated both by its impact at the community level and by the kind of organization it is becoming in the process. Does this intervention lead to greater participation and local ownership, transformed relationships, and increased witness to the gospel? Alternatively, does the program consolidate control at the highest levels of staff, compromise effectiveness, and turn staff members into instruments? For Christian NGOs committed to TD, the temptation to conform to external expectations at the cost of their identity and mission should be resisted. Strategy and mission are not in conflict—TD mission must shape and direct strategy, not the other way around. Strategy should be guided by prayer and shaped by the values of the kingdom. Only then can planning and posture become tools for faithful presence and transformational impact.

MANAGING FOR RESULTS: METRICS AND THEIR LIMITS

In many Christian organizations engaged in Transformational Development (TD), strategy, program design, monitoring, evaluation, and reporting are structured through requirements and processes intended to ensure alignment, accountability, reputation, and impact. While well-intentioned, these systems often follow a top-down logic that may limit flexibility

3. Courtney et al, "Strategy Under Uncertainty," 73–74.

and local agency. Below are some common elements in the strategy to programming cascade:

- Strategy refers to the organization's overarching plan to achieve its goals and fulfill its mission.
- A Strategy Dashboard is a high-level visual tool that helps leadership and management monitor performance against strategic objectives—functioning like a control panel for the organization.
- Program Design translates strategy and donor priorities into detailed operational plans, and it includes logical framework, monitoring and evaluation frameworks, and budget.
- The Logical Framework (logframe) is a structured matrix that outlines project goals, outcomes, outputs, and activities showing how they connect and how results will be measured.
- Monitoring ensures that activities are on track by collecting and analyzing information throughout the program cycle to inform management decisions.
- Evaluations measure the success and impact of programs and progress toward national strategic objectives and targets, with the objective of improving program effectiveness, increasing accountability, and advocating for change.
- Key Performance Indicators (KPIs) are standardized, specific, measurable metrics used to assess progress and performance.

The overall model is shaped by the tools mentioned above, along with others, which are all rooted in a "managing for results" paradigm, emphasizing performance and management control. Their strength is in providing clarity and alignment, but they can also risk marginalizing community perspectives and flattening complex, relational development work into narrow numerical outputs. The diagram that follows illustrates how these systems often cascade from global leadership to community-level implementation, with strategy and programming directions flowing downward and performance data flowing upward—a dynamic that requires critical reflection in light of TD principles.

Diagram 3.1—Strategy to Programming Cascade

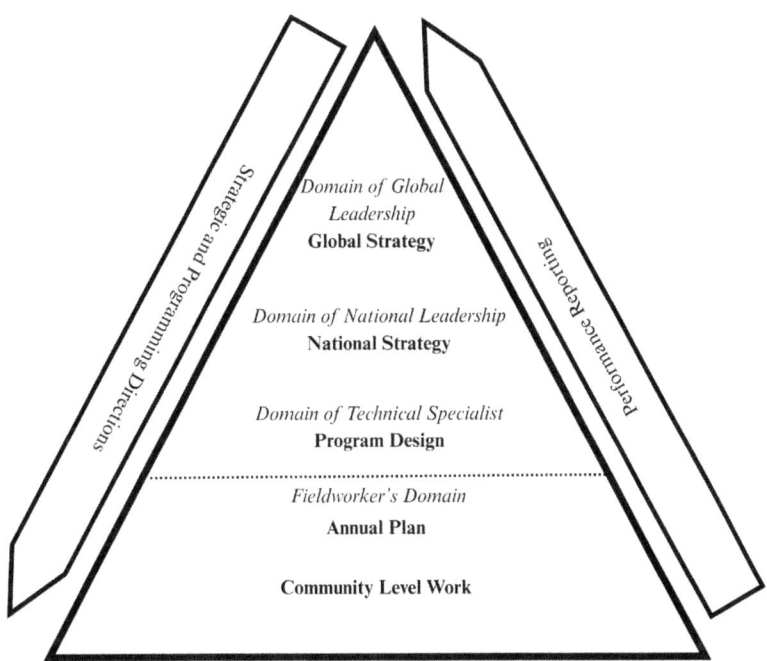

This diagram illustrates the dominant strategic model used by many Christian organizations that claim to pursue Transformational Development. In this model, strategic direction flows from the top-down—from global leadership through national strategy, technical program design, and field-level annual plans—which ultimately shapes the work done at the community level. Each layer reflects a domain of control, with fieldworkers positioned at the bottom as implementers of predefined plans. Meanwhile, the imperative to report results flows bottom-up, as community-level outcomes are translated into performance indicators and channeled back up the hierarchy to satisfy organizational accountability requirements. While many organizations express a desire for monitoring and evaluation processes and KPIs to support learning and adaptation at all levels, the way these processes are typically structured and the assumptions that underpin them often leave little room for local learning, contextual decision-making, and real-time adaptation.

Embedded within this paradigm is a bias toward quantitative and aggregated data, and an implicit belief that such data will naturally surface the right decisions and generate consensus across all levels of the organization. While often well-intentioned, this belief can constrain the faithful embodiment of mission, particularly by overlooking the distinctiveness of local contexts, the need for spiritual discernment, the capacity to navigate uncertainty, and the courage to take relational and programmatic risks.

Though the diagram may appear simplistic, it is deliberately designed to highlight a prevailing strategic posture: one in which planning is centralized, and performance is closely monitored, while local agency, contextual discernment, adaptive learning, and genuine community participation are frequently constrained. This model stands in clear tension with the relational, adaptive, and co-creative ethos of Transformational Development, and raises important questions about how Christian organizations can more faithfully embody their mission in practice.

It is a mistake to assume that tools such as strategy dashboard, logframe, and KPIs–commonly used in managing for results framework–are neutral or universally appropriate. Tools carry embedded assumptions about what matters, how change happens, and what kind of evidence counts. As discussed in the previous chapter, some tools emphasize linear, technical solutions and assume a degree of predictability and standardization that does not reflect the realities of complex, community-based work. For Christian NGOs in particular, these assumptions must be examined theologically. What view of transformation is implied by the organization's primary measurement tools? Do they reinforce managerial control or support relational, Spirit-led practices? The uncritical use of results-based tools risks narrowing an organization's imagination. Overemphasizing measurability can subtly distort priorities and lead to a favoring of short-term outputs over long-term impact, efficiency over faithfulness, and quantitative data over lived experience. Numeric targets can become proxies for success, even when they fail to reflect the deeper relational, spiritual, and social changes that Christian development aspires to foster. If Jesus had relied solely on quantitative indicators to report his ministry, the numbers might have sounded impressive, but also a bit absurd!

- Cost of healing one demon-possessed: 2,000 pigs (estimated value: $1 million, at an average cost of $500 per pig). Not cost efficient.
- Discipleship program: 12 recruited, one dropped out—91.7 percent retention rate.

- Mass feeding event: 5,000 men (not counting women and children) fed with five loaves and two fish. Extremely low cost per beneficiary.
- Miraculous beverage service: 120 gallons of premium wine created instantly. One hundred percent customer satisfaction. No budget impact.

While technically accurate, these figures miss the real story. They do not describe the dignity restored to the man set free from demonic possession, the transformation of ordinary fishermen into bold witnesses, or the joy at a wedding feast celebration. The humor here points to a serious limitation of many development metrics: numbers can track activity, but they often miss the meaning. In Jesus' case, the most powerful moments could not be quantified. Likewise, in Christian development work, measuring only what fits neatly on a dashboard means overlooking the deeper work of hope, faith, and love unfolding quietly in people's lives.

Many measurement tools implicitly assume that only quantitative data can provide deep, objective insight. But data is never self-interpreting. Without space for dialogue and discernment, organizations may miss what the numbers actually mean, or worse, they might assume that the numbers tell the whole story. Effective strategy and monitoring require listening to the data in context: engaging field staff, community partners, and local knowledge to interpret meaning, question assumptions, and uncover blind spots. In this sense, learning must precede judgment. Numbers should provoke inquiry and not justify conclusions. This is especially true in domains such as spiritual formation, community trust, reconciliation, or the deepening of faith. Transformative change is especially difficult to discern through quantitative data. Christian NGOs must take seriously the possibility that tools designed to deliver clarity and control can, when misapplied, limit attentiveness to the slow, complex, relational work that lies at the heart of transformational development. In Bryant Myers's words, "transformation is not about fixing problems, it is about healing relationships."[4]

Fieldworkers often find themselves caught in a persistent tension. They are expected to report progress almost exclusively in numerical terms and to use tools and indicators they had little or no role in designing. Some describe this experience as "working in two languages": one tailored for their head office and the other that resonates with their community. This

---

4. Myers, *Walking with the Poor*, 173.

duality can inhibit meaningful engagement with local communities and impede fieldworkers' ability to monitor impact in locally meaningful ways. As a result, fieldworkers cannot then adapt approaches to align better with broader strategic or missional priorities. This dissonance contributes to frustration, cynicism, and burnout over the course of a career. Other results may not be visible to external observers. Evaluation vocabulary must account for faithfulness as well as fruitfulness. In summary, managing for results has value, but it must be held within a broader vision and mission. Christian NGOs must ask not only "What did we achieve?" but also "Who did we become?" and "Were we faithful to God's calling?" Program evaluation should ask these questions, rather than silence them, to support rather than hinder transformational development.

Artifacts of Evidence

When NGO evaluation entails managing for results, they must produce what Rosalind Eyben, a development anthropologist, calls "artifacts of evidence."[5] Logic models (such as logframes), which underpin much of this approach, rely on evidence chains that begin with collecting data on individual participants such as those who attend meetings or engage in specific program activities. This data typically focuses on measurable attributes linked to particular activities and measures the anticipated changes resulting from participation. This data is captured as numerical values for quantitative indicators, which are then aggregated and compared against pre-established targets. The evidence chain, maintained through detailed forms, metrics, and units of measurement, sustains the logic model's internal coherence. Fieldworkers carry out activities and collect data. Unmet targets reflect poorly on the field level and are seen as a failure of implementation or measurement. Rarely does anyone critically attend to questions of whether the logic model itself appropriately fits the complexities of the change process in a local context or community dynamics.

Fieldworkers find themselves facing an ethical dilemma. How can they foster genuine participation when implementing a plan that offers limited space for community input? While participation may be possible in some tactical aspects of plan implementation, technical specialists at the central office have determined the plan's overall direction. John Dickie Montgomery, a political scientist and scholar, refers to this paradox as

5. Eyben et al., *Politics of Evidence*, 6–8.

bureaucratic populism, a dynamic in which participation does not intend to empower people but to create the appearance that a community has been engaged enough to warrant receiving development assistance.[6] Bureaucratic populism stages or simulates enough local involvement to satisfy institutional expectations all the while maintaining centralized control over decision-making processes. Participation in this framing becomes a performance requirement rather than a transformative process. Even in Christian NGOs that are involved in TD, where participation is theologically framed as essential to transformational development, the weight of organizational control and donor compliance can shift practices toward bureaucratic populism. For example, in a program serving displaced communities in East Africa, fieldworkers shared how community consultations were often held just days before the launch of major activities primarily to fulfill reporting requirements. Project personnel asked local leaders to "endorse" the plans made by outsiders, so that the project leaders could claim that it had been community driven. One fieldworker reflected that this "checklist participation" left her disillusioned, particularly when community members began to ask why they were not consulted earlier.

Eyben offers a helpful conceptual lens to understand this divide between development as officially framed and actually practiced. She contrasts "substantialism," which sees development as a set of discrete outputs and results, with "relationalism," which sees development as unfolding through patterns, processes, and relationships.[7] Many field staff, she notes, officially operate within a substantialist worldview because organizations and donors expect measurable outputs. Nevertheless, informally, and often privately, they prefer relationalist practices. She describes these staff members as "closet relationalists": people who sustain the illusion of structured, measurable development by quietly investing in the unmeasurable relational work that makes those structures function. Their unseen labor, occurring beneath the iceberg, keeps programs running, even if these efforts go unrecognized by performance management systems. This duality between public compliance and private adaptation may help explain how many organizations deliver measurable substantialist results which are enabled by a human relational approach at the field level. As Ben Ramalingam notes, the coexistence of parallel cultures within NGOs (one managerial and visible and the other relational and hidden),

---

6. Montgomery, *Bureaucrats and People*, 4.
7. Eyben, "Hiding Relations," 380–94.

can strain fieldworkers, especially those deeply committed to the ideals of transformational development.[8] These staff members end up working beyond their job descriptions and outside official frameworks; they put in long hours of unpaid and often invisible work to make rigid systems more humane. One fieldworker in a South Indian context recounted how she regularly adjusted program delivery to accommodate cultural festivals, local grievances, and family dynamics, none of which the official workplan considered. To meet both relational expectations and managerial deadlines, she often worked weekends and late nights. These extra efforts were not recorded, let alone rewarded, but she considered them essential for maintaining the integrity of her work with the community. Her story is not uncommon in many Christian NGOs, where staff quietly mediates between official policies and local people.

If Christian NGOs are to remain true to their mission, they would recognize and value this hidden labor. Organizational structures need to be reimagined to reposition management tools as support mechanisms rather than controls and to create space for authentic relational practice. Development is not just about delivering measurable outcomes; it is about walking with people in ways that honor their dignity, complexity, and agency. Recognizing the limitations of our artifacts of evidence is the first step in making room for a more faithful and transformative way of working.

HOW QUANTITATIVE DATA CAN SERVE ORGANIZATIONAL STRATEGY

I want to be clear that my critique is not a dismissal of quantitative data in transformational development. On the contrary, I recognize its important role. Quantitative data plays a vital role in informing and supporting organizational strategy, particularly in tracking the "progress" dimensions of development—those external, observable changes that can be counted and compared over time. This includes physical indicators like infrastructure or crop yield, economic performance, service delivery outputs, and population-level changes in health, education, or employment. Because these aspects can be measured and analyzed, they provide valuable insights into trends, help identify gaps, and inform resource allocation across sectors such as health, agriculture, education, and livelihoods. When thoughtfully selected, these indicators enable organizations to monitor

---

8. Ramalingam, *Aid on the Edge of Chaos*, 86.

progress, compare results across regions, and communicate results clearly to donors, partners, and stakeholders.

However, challenges arise when quantitative data is used to measure complex, relational, or spiritual dimensions of transformational change through numbers alone. A heavy reliance on the managing-for-results paradigm can lead to environments where field staff are expected to report against standardized metrics, even when those metrics fail to capture local realities. While organizations often affirm that "data should be used by everyone," in practice, such data often serves centralized reporting needs more than local learning, which limits meaningful engagement and decision-making by those closest to the communities.

When used appropriately, however, quantitative data becomes a diagnostic tool, offering clarity and direction. For instance, in a child development program in East Africa, tracking malnutrition rates revealed a seasonal spike. While initially assumed to be due to food insecurity, deeper analysis—prompted by the data—revealed that mothers were temporarily migrating for harvest labor, leaving children in the care of siblings who lacked knowledge on proper feeding. This discovery led to targeted caregiver support interventions. The insight began with data but was completed through local dialogue and contextual understanding.

To serve strategy well, quantitative data must be paired with qualitative insight and grounded in local experience. When frontline staff and communities participate in defining what to measure and how to interpret it, metrics become meaningful tools for learning rather than instruments of control. In this way, data becomes a servant to strategy, contributing to discernment, adaptation, and faithful practice in pursuit of transformational outcomes.

CASE STUDY: MEASURING TRANSFORMATIONAL DEVELOPMENT

Here is a case study from my time with World Vision, drawn from the period between 2000 and 2015 when the organization was actively working to define, operationalize, and measure Transformational Development.[9] I had the privilege of providing leadership, along with others, for much of what is described here, and so I bear some responsibility for both its contributions and its limitations. I believe this case study offers valuable

9. Byworth et al., "Transformational Development Indicators Field Guide," 9.

insights for organizations seeking to translate high-level principles of TD into practice and to measure changes in alignment with its vision of holistic transformation.

Defining Transformational Development

World Vision defined TD as a process through which children, families, and communities move toward wholeness of life with dignity, justice, peace, and hope. Building on this definition, a community of practice, made up of practitioners and leaders in World Vision, identified key characteristics of their Transformational Development framework—emphasizing a community-based, holistic, child-focused, and sustainable approach. This framework recognized that development is rarely linear, and it is often disrupted by conflict, disasters, or pandemics. The TD framework viewed enhancing community resilience as integral to the transformational process. A strategic turning point came in 2003 when the organization rolled out a set of Transformational Development Indicators (TDIs). It included quantitative indicators to measure progress dimensions of development such as access to safe water, management of childhood diseases, nutritional status of children, and access to education. It also incorporated qualitative dimensions of change, including increased care for others, the emergence of hope within communities, active community participation, the sustainability of community-based organizations, household resilience, staff spiritual formation, church relations, Christian witness, and a reduction in extreme poverty—as defined by the communities themselves. These indicators became the basis for measuring more complex aspects of transformation. The aim was to standardize the measurements across approximately sixteen hundred programs in more than sixty countries. Through this effort, the organization attempted to translate complex spiritual and social changes into observable and reportable metrics.

Design Principles Behind the TDIs

Five core principles guided the design of TDIs:

1. *Focus on Key Indicators*: TDIs were limited to a manageable set of indicators that could give leadership a high-level view of program strength without delving into in-depth diagnostics.

2. *Show Trends over Time*: TDI measurements were intended to be repeated every three years to enable trend analysis and to track long-term community change.

3. *Support Local Programming*: Although developed at the global level, the Transformational Development Indicators (TDIs) were intended to inform and complement local planning and community engagement, not to dictate program content. The TDIs were aligned with some of the common programming elements from the Transformational Development framework. They were also field-tested and validated in real-world contexts to ensure their relevance and applicability on the ground.

4. *Steward Resources Wisely*: Data collection was to be cost-effective and not burdensome in order to ensure that measurement efforts would not detract from program delivery.

5. *Measure What Matters*: Perhaps most boldly, TDIs included qualitative indicators of intangible outcomes such as hope, caring relationships, spiritual nurture, church partnerships, and Christian witness, alongside standard quantitative metrics on health, nutrition, and education.

This approach represented a bold strategic move. Measuring such intangible changes was rare in mainstream development practice; however, the organization believed that its mission required assessing realities at the heart of transformation and not just material metrics.

Operationalizing Measurement in Practice

Programs collected both quantitative and qualitative data. Quantitative indicators (e.g., child malnutrition, school enrollment, and others) could be aggregated across countries and regions. The heart of the TDIs lay in qualitative measures, gathered through tools such as focus groups, staff reflections, participatory learning activities, and document reviews. These qualitative indicators were scored locally, often using community-generated criteria. They provided valuable insights into how people perceived change: Did they feel more hopeful about their future? How were the community members growing in their resiliency? How were people caring for each other, especially for the most vulnerable? Were children able to participate in decisions that affected them? Were churches more engaged in community transformation? However, a dilemma arose in that these insights were contextual and could not be easily compared across programs. While rich in local meaning, these qualitative findings were difficult to use at national or global levels for comparison, funding decisions, strategic planning, or donor reporting.

The introduction of TDIs impacted fieldworkers and encouraged them to reflect more deeply on community dynamics, spiritual growth, and relationships. Instead of focusing on service delivery or more easily measurable progress, the field staff became more aware of qualitative signs of transformation and were reminded to integrate reflection on spiritual growth and relational dynamics into monitoring routines. Despite its visionary intention, World Vision discontinued the TDI initiative after a span of six years for two main reasons:

1. *Attribution Challenges*: TDIs captured the status of transformational development in communities, but the changes could not be directly attributed to the organization or its program interventions. It became difficult to justify investment in the TDI measurement system when it was not directly related to its work.

2. *Aggregation Limits*: The context-specific nature of qualitative indicators made them valuable locally but unsuitable for the kinds of standardized reporting required at regional or global levels.

Ultimately, the effort to define and measure the "unmeasurable" produced valuable organizational insights and renewed attention to spiritual and relational dimensions of change. However, it also revealed the limitations of universal, qualitative frameworks in capturing complex, lived transformation. As a result, the organization reverted to standard quantitative indicators, those that could be measured, reported, and aggregated, regardless of context. Qualitative and transformational changes were left out.

Broader Lessons from the TDI Experience

The experience of implementing—and eventually discontinuing—the Transformational Development Indicators (TDIs) offers valuable lessons for organizations seeking to measure complex forms of change that cannot be fully captured through numbers or directly attributed to the organization:

1. *Be clear on what and why you measure:* Not everything that matters can be measured, and not everything that is measured matters equally. Organizations should be clear about the purpose of measurement—whether it is for learning, accountability, advocacy, or strategic decision-making—and align their tools accordingly.

2. *Value local meaning over global use:* Context-specific indicators rooted in community perspectives can offer deep insights into transformation at the local level, even if they are not easily aggregated and used. Organizations should resist the temptation to prioritize comparability, global aggregation and use, at the cost of local relevance.

3. *Balance accountability with learning:* Measurement systems should serve both accountability and learning. When data collection becomes a burden or a source of pressure, it can undermine trust, creativity, and responsiveness at the field level. A more balanced approach values feedback and adaptation alongside performance tracking.

4. *Invest in qualitative capacity:* Qualitative data can reveal dimensions of change, such as shifts in relationships, hope, or faith, that numbers alone cannot capture. Collecting qualitative data requires training, tools, and time. Organizations wanting to take transformational development seriously should invest in the capacity to collect and interpret such data.

5. *Anticipate the limits of attribution:* Not all positive change can or should be attributed directly to program interventions. In complex systems, transformation often results from multiple overlapping influences. Acknowledging these realities can lead to more honest reporting and humbler, partnership-oriented practices.

6. *Keep space for experimentation:* Innovative frameworks like the TDIs offer learning opportunities even when they fall short. Rather than seeing such initiatives as failures, organizations can treat them as experiments that surface deeper questions about purpose, evidence, and mission.

None of the lessons outlined above are likely to surprise those familiar with transformational development in practice. Many organizations working in the field have encountered the challenges of collecting qualitative data. Yet the same mistakes are often repeated, as organizations are driven by the powerful allure of being able to measure, aggregate, and report transformational changes so that an organization can claim them as its own achievement. The desire for clarity, control, and credibility can unintentionally overshadow the more complex, relational, and often unmeasurable nature of true transformation.

THE EFFECT OF MONITORING ON FIELDWORKERS

This section draws on my 2017 and 2018 field research conducted within World Vision programs in Tamil Nadu, South India.[10] The study explored the tensions experienced by NGO fieldworkers, the discretion they exercised, and the coping mechanisms they developed in response. What follows is a summary of the specific tensions fieldworkers faced regarding the timely execution of pre-planned activities and program monitoring requirements, as they relate to the topic under discussion in this chapter.

Program managers, those who supervised fieldworkers, viewed success primarily through the lens of performance against targets and financial execution, particularly the timely spending of budgets. These supervisors believed that high expectations would drive productivity; timely outputs and expenditures would contribute to the organization's goal of improvements in child well-being; consistent delivery would help sustain donor funding; and, importantly, the ambitious targets could be achieved. Accordingly, as fieldworkers struggled to meet these expectations, there was little room for empathy. Performance management systems reinforced this approach by assessing more favorably the completion of pre-planned activities, achievement of numerical outputs, and timely reporting. By contrast, deep community engagement and responsiveness to emergent needs received far less organizational weight or oversight. Salary increments and performance ratings were tied to measurable results, not to qualitative or relational outcomes.

The emphasis on metrics affected fieldworkers in several ways. On the one hand, numerical targets gave them a defensible framework for their work and a way to navigate accountability pressures. Knowing they had followed required procedures gave them a sense of protection, but it also made them more risk averse. At the same time, the focus on outputs made their roles increasingly task-oriented and limited the space for relational engagement and adaptive responses. Most fieldworkers understood the importance of targets and acknowledged that without clear metrics,

10. Sarma, "Experience of Fieldworkers," 132–52.

supervisors could judge their work arbitrarily. Yet they also lamented the limited time left for building relationships in the community. Their days were filled with scheduled activities, coordination tasks, and administrative obligations. As a result, opportunities for unplanned conversations, exploration of emerging needs, or deeper relational presence, which are critical for transformational development, were rare.

Many field staff experienced the development approach as increasingly transactional, based on how it was measured by these outputs. The emphasis on quantifiable measurable outputs and financial compliance meant the deeper and more significant changes in people's lives received less focused attention in day-to-day work. Organizational leaders maintained that delivering the designed evidence-based outputs would lead to broader transformational outcomes. However, fieldworkers found it difficult to see or substantiate these connections. Their proximity to community realities gave field staff insight into local complexity, but the organization's emphasis on targets and timelines did not reflect this reality. Few fieldworkers fully understood why pre-planned targets had to be met so strictly or why underspending budgets raised concern. They did not see the institutional pressures their managers faced from funding offices that equated underspending with inefficiency and unmet targets as evidence of poor performance.

The disconnect between the world of the fieldworkers (rooted in relationships, responsiveness, and constant adaptation) and the world of management (structured around planning frameworks, logframes, strategy dashboards, KPIs, and funding cycles) created ongoing tension. Some fieldworkers expressed concern that emphasizing measurable results risked reducing transformational development to a series of deliverables. Progress indicators could not reliably measure meaningful change, and relying on standardized metrics could misrepresent actual impact in dynamic settings where constantly changing conditions necessitated the real-time adaptation of interventions, as opposed to a standardized roll out. The lines between actions and outcomes could not always be connected. For example, in a program addressing child malnutrition in rural India, field staff reported that official metrics tracked the distribution of nutrition supplements, but the real breakthroughs came from addressing local problems like alcoholism, gender norms, and land access. The focus on quantifiable results, especially short-term outputs (e.g., the number of nutrition supplements distributed), obscured the field staff's work on the local problems that stood in the way of the desired deeper, long-term transformation.

This dilemma underscores a central tension in strategy-driven program design and implementation. When short-term deliverables define organizational effectiveness, it can diminish focus on the slower, adaptive, and relational processes through which deep and lasting transformation actually occurs. As the next section shows, this tension becomes even more acute when field staff address complex challenges in contexts of low predictability. There, rigid strategies and standardized tools are most at risk of missing what communities need most.

TECHNICAL RATIONALITY AND BOTTOM-UP APPROACHES

One of the key tensions of transformational development lies in deciding when to apply standardized, evidence-based best practices, and when to allow for more adaptive, context-specific solutions. Not all development challenges are created equal. Some lend themselves to more straightforward, technical solutions that can be implemented consistently across different settings, while others are deeply embedded in social, cultural, and relational dynamics and so require greater sensitivity, discretion, and local adaptation. The challenge for organizations is not to choose one approach over the other but to show wisdom to discern which approach fits the problem at hand. In his book *Navigation by Judgment*, author Dan Honig provides a useful framework for navigating this tension. He proposes two criteria that organizations can use to decide between a centralized, standardized approach and a decentralized, judgment-based strategy, namely project verifiability and environmental predictability.[11]

Project verifiability refers to how tightly linked a project's quantifiable outputs are to its ultimate outcomes and goals. When the connection between deliverables and desired change is clear and strong (e.g., distributing vaccines to prevent disease or applying fertilizers to increase agricultural yield), then using standardized, technical solutions is appropriate. These projects are typically found in the biological, medical, and physical sciences, where causal relationships are well established. However, the link between outputs and long-term transformation is far more tenuous for transformational development projects related to behavior issues, social

11. Honig, *Navigation by Judgment*, 8–10.

norms, community participation, and faith-based values. Outcomes that cannot be easily attributed to specific activities require a different approach.

Honig's second criterion, environmental predictability, refers to the stability and comprehensibility of the context in which a project operates. A predictable environment allows planners to anticipate risks and to plan accordingly. However, in many fragile, marginalized, or informal settings where Christian NGOs work, the environment can be unpredictable. Unexpected shocks (i.e., economic downturns, political instability, natural disasters, or social unrest) can rapidly alter the development landscape. Moreover, even within relatively stable countries, localized environments like informal urban settlements can present volatile conditions that challenge outsiders' understanding and control. Highly centralized pre-planned strategies will be less effective in more unpredictable environments.

What then should organizations do when faced with low project verifiability and low environmental predictability, which, as it turns out, are often characteristic of the areas where the poorest and most vulnerable live? Organizations should not abandon strategy altogether, but they can create space for shared ownership, adaptation, and field-level learning. This means requiring and rewarding the ongoing learning processes of frontline workers and community members throughout project implementation. In such settings, responsiveness, humility, and mutual discernment are as essential as formal plans. Organizational leaders can draw on promising practices where they exist but also encourage program teams, including fieldworkers, to adapt those models to their context. Fieldworkers must not be treated merely as implementers of centrally designed projects; they have intimate knowledge of their communities and their lived realities. One way to access field staff's context expertise is by joining specialists' technical expertise with fieldworkers' contextual expertise to co-create program designs. The technical interventions that form a project's backbone should be complemented by more flexible, relational, and often context specific activities that respond to a community's unique needs and aspirations. These activities could include efforts to strengthen local leadership, change community members' behavior, foster spiritual reflection, or address hidden vulnerabilities, such as gender-based violence or social exclusion. While these activities are harder to measure, they are often central to achieving true transformational outcomes.

Organizations can and should still hold project teams accountable for outcomes in areas where the environment is unpredictable and the links between outputs and goals is not as strong (project verifiability), but the focus of accountability should shift. Rather than emphasizing strict adherence to pre-determined outputs or timelines, organizations should assess whether teams are making thoughtful, informed adaptations that align with and contribute to the achievement of outcome-level goals. In this way, fieldworkers are encouraged to navigate using the outcomes as a compass rather than to implement a fixed recipe of pre-determined activities and processes. Encouraging iterative learning and reflection, especially when paired with local monitoring and community feedback, can help ensure that projects remain faithful to their transformational mission even in unpredictable environments. Simple, evidence-based solutions have their place, particularly when the path from action to outcome is clear and replicable. But most real-world contexts require a hybrid approach that balances technical rationality with adaptive, relational engagement. This is not only a more realistic way of working, but it is also more aligned with the core principles of transformational development.

EVALUATIONS: PRINCIPLES FOR MEASURING KINGDOM IMPACT

As mentioned earlier, evaluations measure the success and impact of programs, as well as progress toward the planned objectives. They are typically conducted once every three to five years. How do we discern and document meaningful change that reflects the fullness of God's redemptive work? Conventional approaches to evaluation, which focus on outcomes, impact, and accountability, have value but often fail to capture spiritual transformation, restored relationships, or deep shifts in values and identity. These intangible outcomes, central to the TD's mission, require a different posture and set of tools. Emerging approaches suggest a movement toward measuring with the heart as well as the head, rooted in theological reflection, community discernment, and relational engagement. Evaluation of transformation in Christian development work must move beyond a narrow focus on program outcomes and impact at a tangible level. Scholar practitioners like Mark Harden,[12] Frank Cookingham,[13] and Subodh Kumar[14] identify several noteworthy principles:

12. Harden, "Faith-Based Program Theory," 481–504.
13. Cookingham, "Transformative Evaluation."
14. Kumar, "Kingdom Impact," 24–36.

1. *Ground Evaluation in Theological Purpose*: The starting point of evaluation must be a clear biblical vision of transformation. Measurements should reflect our understanding that God desires reconciliation, justice, restored relationships, and spiritual formation, not just improved services or increased reach.

2. *Prioritize Long-Term and Transformational Outcomes*: Kingdom impact unfolds over time. Evaluations must be designed to demonstrate long-term effects that include changes in hope, resilience, social trust, or local leadership—not just near-term outputs.

3. *Embed Reflexive and Spiritual Practices*: Evaluation should be treated as a spiritual discipline as well as a technical task. Practices like prayer, Scripture reflection, and community discernment should accompany data collection and analysis to invite God's voice and honor community wisdom.

4. *Engage Local Interpretation of Data*: Numerical data should not be treated as self-explanatory or as accessible to outside experts only. Fieldworkers and community members must be engaged in interpreting what the data actually means locally. This helps evaluators to avoid false conclusions and ensures that analysis reflects lived realities.

5. *Affirm the Vocational Role of Fieldworkers*: Acknowledge and honor the reality that field-level staff are more than data collectors; their embeddedness in the community gives them insight into how spiritual and relational change is unfolding. Their discernment must be recognized as a valid and vital form of knowledge.

6. *Use Evaluation as a Tool for Learning and Witness*: Instead of judgment, evaluation becomes a means to testify and a safe place to learn from failures and name what God is doing—seen and unseen—through the journey of community transformation.

Together, these principles reflect a shift from measuring solely for accountability to measuring for transformation. Rather than extracting evidence to prove success, evaluation becomes a spiritual discipline, providing a space for noticing what God is doing, celebrating unseen fruit, acknowledging unfinished work, and being reshaped in the process. In a Christian NGO program in Southeast Asia, an internal evaluation found that while school attendance and household income had increased, a deeper transformation meant that people began to express renewed hope. Instead of treating this insight as anecdotal, the team held listening sessions with field staff, church leaders, and women's groups to understand what "hope" looked like in their context. They discovered it meant families choosing to stay in the village instead of migrating, greater participation in local church leadership by women, and new expressions of solidarity across communal divisions. These measurements—of families not migrating, of women in church leadership, and of solidarity—became new indicators for tracking relational, spiritual, and contextualized progress and for showing how numerical growth intersected with kingdom values.

ALIGNING STRATEGY WITH MISSION AND THE MOVEMENT OF THE SPIRIT

One of the tensions in Christian NGOs today lies between the demands of strategic management and the unpredictable, relational, Spirit-led nature of transformational development. Strategies are inherently forward-looking and goal oriented. They rely on logic, forecasting, and measurable outcomes. Yet the mission of God requires attentiveness to what is emergent, relational, and Spirit-led. Aligning strategy with the TD mission means holding organizational planning and execution in an attitude of discernment and learning. It means resisting the impulse to treat strategy as a rigid blueprint and instead to approach it as a flexible guide shaped by prayer, humility, and ongoing listening. As Chris Wright reminds us, the mission of God is not something we manage; it is something we join.[15] This alignment begins with theological clarity. Christian NGOs must continuously revisit the foundational questions: What is our mission? How do we define transformation? What do we believe about human dignity, sin, reconciliation, and hope? These convictions must not be relegated to mission statements alone. They must animate planning cycles, budgeting processes, and other operational aspects. Begin strategy development with prayer retreats and communal discernment exercises, and anchor decisions in Scripture and reflection. Convene "listening forums" where staff and partners share where they sense God is moving in their contexts and use the themes as a compass for planning. Aligning with mission also requires space for interruption. The Spirit often moves outside of our plans through unexpected crises, new partnerships, or prophetic insights from the

15. Wright, *Mission of God*, 22.

margins. Organizations must create margins for such holy disruptions. As Bryant Myers notes, transformational development is more about faithful presence than flawless plans.[16]

A Spirit-aligned strategy is still disciplined, but it is also humble. It allows for failure, ambiguity, and mystery. It embraces the slow, patient work of formation and trust-building. It sees communities not as targets but as collaborators in God's redemptive story. Practically, aligning strategy with mission involves ongoing reflection and adaptation. It calls for regular cycles of learning, spiritual examination, and communal prayer. Leaders must model this posture by remaining open to feedback, curious about local insights, and willing to reimagine long-held assumptions. Finally, alignment with the Spirit requires courage. Sometimes the mission of God will challenge institutional self-interest, donor preferences, or mainstream development norms. A truly faithful strategy will not always be marketable, but it will be prophetic. It will bear witness not only to what we do, but to who we are and whose we are.

The challenge is not just to do strategy differently; it is to become a different kind of people. Culture change is slow, but it begins with the stories we tell, the values we live, and the leadership we embody. In the end, the best strategic plan is not one that achieves the most, but one that most deeply reflects who God is and how God works. In Christian NGOs, leadership is not just about outcomes. It is about forming communities of grace, integrity, and courage, so that the strategy itself becomes an expression of witness.

FIELDWORKER AT THE CROSSROADS OF STRATEGY, M&E, AND COMMUNITY ENGAGEMENT

As we conclude the chapter, I'd like to bring together key themes we have explored and offer a vision of an ideal scenario. The way Christian organizations design their strategy and implement monitoring and evaluation (M&E) systems affects how well they live out their mission and values. The diagram below illustrates an ideal scenario in which strategy and M&E are not imposed top-down but shaped and reshaped through a dynamic relationship between the organization, the community, and the fieldworker who inhabits the space between them.

---

16. Myers, *Walking with the Poor*, 232.

Transformational Frontiers

Diagram 3.2—Ideal Scenario of Fieldworker Mediating Strategy and M&E

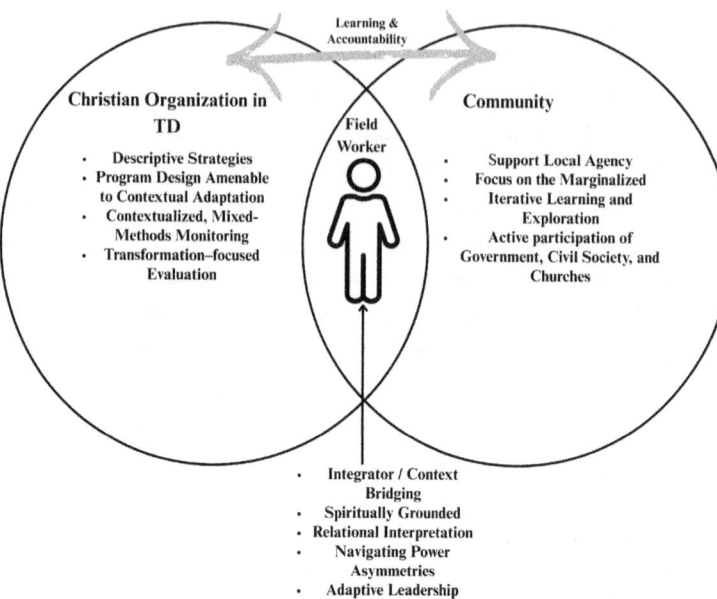

On the organizational side, effective strategy and M&E in TD begins with descriptive strategies—not prescriptive blueprints, but directional commitments that leave space for local discernment. Fieldworkers adapt program designs and shape implementation based on frontline realities. They are also able to contextualize monitoring systems, incorporating both quantitative and qualitative indicators that capture globally standardized measures where appropriate, as well as locally relevant dimensions. Evaluations focus on transformation and seek to understand both the change occurring and the answer to the question Who are we becoming? We must also ask how and why the changes are occurring and whether the changes align with kingdom values.

On the community side, transformational development requires supporting local agency, prioritizing the marginalized, and creating space for iterative learning, exploration, and active participation from churches and faith-based organizations, civil society, and local government. These principles affirm that transformation emerges from within, in response to both material realities and spiritual beliefs.

At the center of this relationship stands the fieldworker. More than an implementer of pre-determined interventions, the fieldworker is an integrator and context bridge builder, who is tasked with translating organizational intentions into locally meaningful action and bringing community insights and challenges back to the organization. Their role requires them to have a posture of spiritual groundedness, the capacity for relational interpretation, and the ability to navigate power asymmetries with humility and wisdom. Fieldworkers constantly adapt in response to shifting realities, all while holding in tension their commitment to the community and to the organization in tension.

The two-way arrow at the top of the diagram reflects the vital processes of learning and accountability, that flows in both directions: from the organization to the community in the form of guidance and support, and from the community to the organization through grounded feedback, insights, and reflection. When properly supported, fieldworkers help facilitate this two-way flow and ensure that M&E systems are not extractive, but generative—tools for collective learning, not just performance measurement. This diagram offers a vision of strategy and M&E that supports, rather than constrains, transformational development. It is idealistic. This model calls us to reimagine how strategy and M&E might truly serve the mission—to act justly, love mercy, and walk humbly with God in the work of transformation.

BEARING FRUIT THAT LASTS: STRATEGY AS WITNESS

Strategic planning, program design, monitoring, and evaluation are not merely technical functions within Christian NGOs; they are deeply theological acts. They reflect what we believe about God, about people, about the nature of transformation, and about our calling in the world. Too often, however, these functions have been shaped more by secular paradigms of efficiency, scale, and measurement than by the gospel's invitation to faithful presence, relational restoration, and Spirit-led discernment. Throughout this chapter, we have explored both the promise and the peril of strategy. When approached with humility and spiritual discernment, strategy can bring clarity, coherence, and wise stewardship of resources. It can keep organizations focused amid complexity and committed to long-term vision. Yet when strategy becomes primarily a response to donor expectations, technocratic logic, or internal managerial control, it risks distorting the mission. It can marginalize fieldworkers, narrow our definition of success, and miss the slow, sacred work of transformation already unfolding in communities. Christian organizations must resist the temptation to equate impact with visibility, efficiency, or numerical growth. Our strategies must instead be shaped by the logic of the kingdom. This means valuing relationships over results, stories over statistics, and faithfulness over scale. Monitoring and evaluation must be reimagined as tools for learning, listening, and testimony, not merely for accountability.

We have seen that honoring fieldworker agency, investing in reflection and discernment, and allowing space for Spirit-led interruption are not peripheral concerns. They are central to the credibility and vitality of Christian witness. At their best, strategic frameworks should reflect the character of Christ followers—patient, hopeful, relational, and just. They must be open to community wisdom, sensitive to context, and grounded in the conviction that God is already at work and graciously invites us to join. In the end, the most enduring fruit of our labor will not be measured in reports or key performance indicators but in lives transformed by love, communities restored in dignity, and organizations that reflect the justice and mercy of our Lord. May we plan, implement, and evaluate with open hands, soft hearts, and listening ears. For in the economy of the kingdom, it is not the most strategic, but it is the most faithful, who bear the fruit that lasts.

4

Evangelism and Church Partnerships Within the Context of Holistic Ministry

The Place of Evangelism in Holistic Ministry

IN THE PREVIOUS CHAPTER, we examined the role of organizational strategy and how it shapes the responsibilities of fieldworkers in program planning, implementation, monitoring, and evaluation within Christian organizations. One key area of tension in strategic planning and program planning, monitoring, and evaluation is how an organization articulates its faith commitment within the context of holistic ministry. Christian organizations involved in holistic ministry often navigate this tension by committing at various levels to a witness in both word and deed with the hope that individuals will come to acknowledge Christ as the Lord of their lives. Large organizations, especially those receiving funds from the public and non-Christian donors, often take a measured and careful approach to evangelism. They may incorporate Christian faith into their organization's life in meaningful ways, such as through mission statements, policies that reflect a holistic vision, chapel services, devotions, and retreats. Similarly, their programming approaches may include collaboration with churches. However, they may retain official organizational policies that intentionally refrain from overt evangelism or formal verbal proclamation of the gospel being mindful of the potential risks to donor funding, compliance with host government regulations, and the need to respect religious diversity.

A sincere concern, shaped by the large scale of their programs, significant budgets, and the vulnerability of the populations they serve, often heightens their caution against imposing, or even appearing to impose, their Christian faith.

The Christian gospel may provide the inspiration and values for social, economic, and material well-being; programs partner with churches as civil society institutions. On the other hand, organizations that maintain evangelism as an integral part of their holistic work may altogether avoid working in contexts or receiving donor funding that would restrict them from sharing the good news of Christ with those that they serve. A truly holistic understanding of development places the desire to make Christ known at its core and integrates the gospel proclamation with efforts to address human needs—while simultaneously remaining faithful to both commitments, even in challenging contexts and amid the complex issues those setting presents. Holistic development does not mean that evangelism is lost or pushed to the background. We cannot separate the call to do good development work, centered on people and responsive to their needs, from the call to point people to Christ as the ultimate source of life. As Bryant Myers states, if the kingdom of God is our understanding of the best future and the end goal of development, then we should earnestly desire, hope, pray, and appropriately witness to the love of God expressed through the birth, life, teachings, death, and resurrection of Jesus Christ.[1]

For holistic ministry to be sustainable, the presence or the emergence of a local community of believers is essential, especially in contexts where none exists. We should always seek to share the love of Christ in incarnational, contextually sensitive, and ethically right ways while also respecting the freedom of people to make their own choices in all areas of life, including their faith. It is important to acknowledge that no matter how context sensitive we are, we will hold in tension the goal of supporting peoples' self-determination in the TD process while also affirming faith in Christ as essential to fullness of life. Fieldworkers experience this tension more than anyone else in a Christian organization. In this chapter we engage with this tension and highlight some ways forward.

Please note that this chapter is primarily written for organizations engaging with predominantly non-Christian or minority-Christian contexts. Fully expressing a Christian spirituality that includes evangelism is less problematic in Christian majority contexts, where it is safe to assume

---

1. Myers, *Walking with the Poor*, 175.

there are Christian community members, churches, and leaders willing to form partnerships. I recognize that there could be other challenges in Christian majority contexts: inter-church conflicts, partiality in the selection of program participants, and even the perception of favoritism among church denominations. Churches' organizational capacity may be limited such that in the long term infusing churches with external resources could become unhealthy. We will consider some of these issues in our discussion of church partnerships. Even so, sharing the good news of God's offer of forgiveness through Jesus Christ in the context of holistic ministry in non-Christian majority contexts presents unique challenges that we will consider in much of this chapter.

TYPOLOGY OF MODELS: INTEGRATING SPIRITUAL ACTIVITIES

Mark G. Harden, a theologian and scholar, proposes a framework to understand better how faith-based organizations integrate spiritual and social/development objectives in program planning and implementation. Recognizing that traditional program theories based on cause effect models often ignore the role of faith in shaping development outcomes, Harden considers the nature of intentionality and spontaneity for integrating spiritual activities to achieve development outcomes.[2]

Intentionality refers to the deliberate, planned inclusion of spiritual activities, such as prayer, Scripture reading, or evangelism, as core components of a program's design and implementation. This approach weaves faith expressions into a program's structure and logic in order to contribute to both spiritual and social transformation. Organizations with high intentionality explicitly align their activities with their theological convictions and treat spiritual activities as integral to achieving their program goals. By contrast, spontaneity describes the unplanned, organic expressions of faith that arise naturally in the course of relationships, interactions, or community engagement. Spontaneous spiritual elements are not formally included in program designs, but they emerge in the daily rhythm of work, through conversations, moments of prayer, or acts of compassion. This approach values openness to the movement of the Holy Spirit and allows space for frontline staff or community members to express faith in contextually appropriate and personally meaningful ways.

2. Harden, "Faith-Based Program Theory," 496–98.

Please note that spontaneity and intentionality are not binary categories; organizations often draw from both depending on the context and the individuals involved. While intentionality typically reflects planned actions at the organizational or programmatic level, spontaneity often emerges through the decisions of individuals or teams responding in the moment and both can exist simultaneously. Drawing on the work of Dr. Mark Harden, the following models illustrate how spiritual activities intersect with program goals, based on the degree of intentionality and spontaneity, and whether these elements are structurally separate or integrated:

1. The *charismatic* model places explicit spiritual activities, such as prayer and evangelism, at the center of transformation with the belief that spiritual outcomes lead to social and material changes.

2. The *enhancement* model makes use of spiritual practices to support social outcomes. Examples may include drawing from Scripture for lessons on reducing violence and promoting harmony in families, protecting children, promoting responsible sexual behavior, and caring for orphans and vulnerable children.

3. The *traditional* model structurally separates spiritual and social components. For example, one arm of a church denomination may focus on development work and others focus on spiritual activities.

4. In the *modern* model, poverty alleviation and development outcomes themselves are understood as part of salvation and spiritual outcomes. The model often minimizes overt spiritual expressions and focuses primarily on professionalized program delivery.

Diagram 4.1—An Adapted Version of Harden's Typology of Integration Models

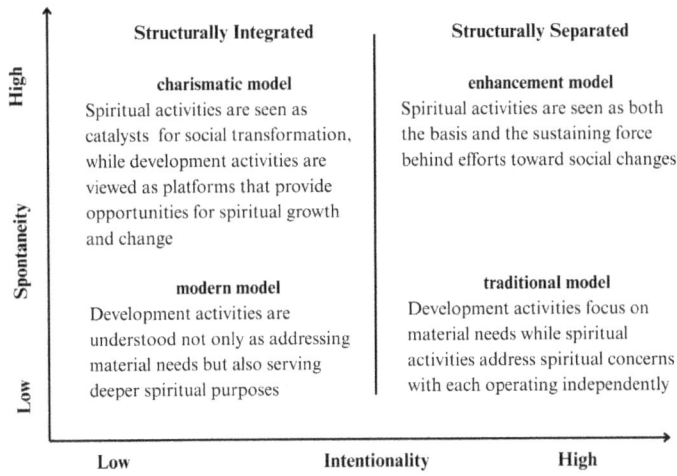

I believe that this typology of faith-based program models, charismatic, enhancement, traditional, and modern, offers important insight into the varied approaches to Christian witness and their implications for fieldworkers. The *Charismatic* model overtly integrates spiritual activities into development work. Fieldworkers embody a fully integrated ministry and engage in both proclamation and service. While this model can lead to bold expressions of witness, it requires cultural sensitivity and deep spiritual maturity to avoid unintended offense or coercion, particularly in pluralistic or religiously sensitive contexts. The *Enhancement* model intentionally includes spiritual practices as supportive of development goals, which creates space for a more balanced and contextualized witness. These settings encourage fieldworkers to live out their faith through relationships, prayer, and servant leadership within programs.

The *Traditional* model maintains a structural separation between spiritual and social components. This model diverges from a holistic understanding of transformational development. Although Christian witness may still occur through church partnerships or parallel ministries, it is not integrated within the development work itself. Fieldworkers in these settings do not have much of a role in spiritual engagement; faith expression is either delegated to others or seen as outside fieldworkers' formal responsibilities. Witness may often be limited to private spaces.

Christian faith may still inspire individuals, but the organization may appear functionally secular in its development work.

In the *modern* model, Christian witness is often minimal or in the background. This model emphasizes professionalism and alignment with secular expectations; spiritual activities are less important than developmental activities. Fieldworkers functioning in *modern* models may feel their spiritual calling is marginalized or must be expressed informally and discreetly. It can promote a quiet, deeply embedded Christian witness, particularly when staff understand the theological meaning of their work and when faith is lived out in action rather than explicit proclamation. This can lead to a sense of vocational dissonance for those who see proclamation as an important part of their ministry. Though the *enhancement* model is structurally separate, it upholds spiritual motivations as fuel for development. It can sustain Christian witness through moral conviction, prayerful support, and integrity, and yet it risks a dualism if spiritual aspects are not visibly connected to the work on the ground. The *Charismatic* model integrates spiritual and development activities with a high degree of spontaneity. It often provides powerful experiences of incarnational witness, prayer, and spiritual openness, especially in grassroots settings. However, it may lack consistency or institutional support for long-term transformation if not grounded in reflection and on the ground support.

Across all models, fieldworkers are best equipped to serve faithfully when the organization clearly articulates its approach to spiritual integration. Regardless of the model, many field staff find ways to live out their faith in context-sensitive, relational ways, through presence, compassion, prayer, and faithful service. Ultimately, the typology reminds us that Christian witness need not be confined to formal structures or strategic plans. It often flows most powerfully through fieldworkers who see their work not just as a profession, but as a calling to bear witness to Christ in both word and deed, through programs and lives deeply rooted in the gospel.

FAITH AND FREEDOM: WHY THE POOR AND OPPRESSED TURN TO CHRIST

Most people do not come to faith in Christ with purely "spiritual" motives in an abstract or otherworldly sense. Faith intertwines with other realities of life; spiritual transformation is not separate from temporal concerns. If it is acceptable for someone to seek Christ for inner peace, healing, or freedom from addiction in the Western contexts, why should it be viewed differently when poor and marginalized people seek Christ as a path to economic dignity and social inclusion? I am not suggesting that we promise economic incentives for people to become Christians—that would be manipulative and would represent both poor Christian witness and poor development practice. However, it is important to recognize the poor genuinely seek Christ for reasons that include liberation from material poverty and social exclusion. The gospel speaks to the whole of life, and it is precisely its capacity to address inner brokenness and to contribute to improved material well-being that makes it good news for the poor.

The idea of dividing life into strictly "spiritual" and "secular" categories is a foreign concept to many, particularly in more traditional worldviews in which faith is not compartmentalized but rather deeply integrated into every aspect of life. Spiritual renewal cannot be separated from material and social well-being. For marginalized communities, spiritual salvation is not merely about the afterlife; salvation fundamentally connects to freedom from oppression, exploitation, and poverty. What is spiritually good must also be good economically, politically, and socially. For these reasons, practices like evangelism, prayer, worship, and teaching the Word of God should be recognized as development assets. These spiritual practices are deeply transformative and bring about significant change at both the individual and community levels.

In the early 1900s, the mass movement of Dalits to Christianity in the Indian subcontinent represented more than a religious conversion. It was a bold step toward reclaiming dignity and breaking free from the oppressive grip of caste-based discrimination that had long defined their social reality. As they found new identity as Christians, their primary motivation was the pursuit of higher social status, personal dignity, and freedom from oppressive landowners. More than one-third of them were convinced spiritually about their choice and a vast majority of them became Christians along with their family and community members.[3]

In a more recent study, missiologist Rupen Das conducted research among Syrian refugees living in Lebanon and slum dwellers in Bangalore, India, who had converted to Christianity from Islam and Hinduism respectively. He says that for poor people who come from other religions, conversion can be a process that takes time as they look beyond themselves and their gods who failed them in the past to a God who is real, hears their

---

3. Pachuau, "Clash of 'Mass Movements'?," 159.

prayers, and cares for them. In Christ they encounter a God who is both transcendent and near to them and answers their prayers. Some individuals would encounter Christ through signs and wonders, in healings, in miraculous provision for their needs, or in finding peace amid conflicts. As the Holy Spirit works in them through regeneration, they learn initial teachings, study Scripture, and fellowship with other believers, and they develop an awareness of their sinfulness and their need for forgiveness through the sacrificial death of Jesus Christ. Individuals may even start attending church gatherings before they come to a saving knowledge of Jesus Christ. Rupen Das identified this pattern for people who had in common experiences of suffering, poverty, and alienation.[4] The process Rupen Das outlines is in contrast to the commonly held expectation in many Western evangelical circles, which often assumes a linear progression, from evangelism to conversion, then discipleship, and finally spiritual growth.

Bryant Myers draws insights from a small number of ethnographic studies conducted in West and East Africa and Central America that focus on the relevance of progressive Pentecostal churches for Christian NGOs working with the poor. The NGOs aligned with Harden's Charismatic model, which places explicit spiritual activities, such as prayer and evangelism, at the center of transformation. Myers highlights how spiritual experiences, such as conversion, baptism in the Holy Spirit, worship, healing, and deliverance, profoundly affect the lives of individuals, families, and communities, and lead to reduced domestic violence, increased sobriety, and more ethical behavior. Christian NGOs can draw on Pentecostals' emphasis on deep personal transformation rooted in the radical redefinition of the identity through which the poor become children of God. This transformation leads to significant shifts in attitude, behavior, and life direction, which all become grounded in a biblical narrative that shapes how people understand God's desire to be actively involved in their lives. These churches promote new moral behaviors that encourage growth and well-being as members reject drinking, partying, and womanizing at the same time they challenge harmful cultural practices and aspects of traditional religion. Notably, these churches are indigenously led and deeply rooted in local language, culture, and worldview; they offer models of development that are both contextually relevant and spiritually grounded.[5]

---

4. Das, *God That the Poor Seek*, 209.
5. Myers, "Progressive Pentecostalism," 115–20.

These spiritual experiences transform one's worldview and reorient their identity and purpose. People are empowered to see themselves not as victims of circumstances or as God-forsaken but as valued and capable individuals created in God's image. Understanding God's purpose for families as central to his design for human flourishing strengthens relationships, mutual responsibility, and support in breaking the cycles of poverty and restoring wholeness in community life. Likewise, embracing work as vocation helps individuals recognize that God has entrusted people with gifts and opportunities to cultivate resources and contribute to their communities. This shift in identity, values, and vocational purpose lays a foundation for lasting economic and social transformation. This empowering biblical worldview provides a strong foundation for doing holistic ministry among the poor and oppressed.

COMMUNICATION OF CHRISTIAN IDENTITY AND MISSION

The Challenge and Perception of Power Imbalance

The Christian faith is historically and inherently missionary in nature. As such, when Christian organizations work in non-Christian communities, there is often an underlying suspicion among community members that development assistance may be tied to proselytism. This is especially acute in post-colonial contexts where outside intervention often carries with it visible and invisible power dynamics, shaped in part by historical collaboration between Christian missions and colonial powers. Outsiders tend to have social capital, technical knowledge, access to funding, and authority—advantages not always shared by the local community members. Furthermore, outside workers can exit the community when tensions arise, while local followers would bear the long-term cost of association with Christianity. For these reasons, it is essential that Christian organizations communicate their identity, values, and mission clearly and thoughtfully, while also nurturing genuine relationships that reflect the very principles they seek to live out. As I will discuss below, it requires wisdom to be transparent about the organization's identity and values without triggering unnecessary suspicions, all the while promoting trust and genuine relationships.

The Myth of Neutrality

Development studies have historically marginalized religion, largely due to the dominant influence of Enlightenment rationalism and modernization theory on the field's foundational assumptions.[6] Secular organizations often view themselves as neutral when it comes to religion and faith and believe they are keeping personal religious beliefs separate from their professional development work. However, this assumption of neutrality is questionable, as secularism itself can function as a worldview with its own set of guiding principles that places science and technology at the center. In reality, all organizations, including secular ones, operate from a particular perspective on poverty, human nature, and the ultimate goal of development. A materialistic worldview, for example, sees poverty primarily as a lack of material resources or education, or as the result of systemic injustice. Accordingly, secular development agencies focus on addressing these issues at the material or structural level and believe that satisfying physical and economic needs will achieve the desired development outcomes. However, this perspective often differs from how people in poor communities understand their own realities and envision their futures. Secular organizations freely share and promote their views among the communities they serve and assume that their approach is more universally acceptable in pluralistic societies. Yet, these perspectives remain largely rooted in Western thought and may, in practice, impose an external framework on communities that have a more holistic understanding of life that integrates material, social, and spiritual dimensions. In many cultures, issues like poverty and illness are understood to be rooted in spiritual causes, although secular development workers tend to dismiss such beliefs as superstitions.

However, in recent years, secular agencies have begun to recognize the role of faith and religious institutions in development more recently. For example, in 2016, the World Bank president acknowledged the vital role of faith-based actors and the importance of integrating moral and spiritual values such as mercy and compassion in order to enhance the effectiveness and reach of development.[7] However, Christian organizations have always understood the centrality of faith in shaping all areas of life. Even as secular agencies have become more open to acknowledging the role of faith and

---

6. Carbonnier, "Religion and Development," 1–4.
7. Taylor, "Mercy."

religious institutions in development, they typically maintain a stance of neutrality and refrain from engagement rooted in personal or institutional faith. Their recognition of faith and spirituality is mostly instrumental, with value insofar as it serves development objectives. This recent endorsement of the role of faith, religion, and spirituality may superficially align with Harden's *modern* model, described earlier in the chapter. By contrast, Christian organizations have long recognized that faith is central to shaping every aspect of life and development.

NAVIGATING TRUST AND TRANSPARENCY

Building trust while remaining transparent presents both an opportunity and a responsibility. To build trust, Christian organizations must be transparent in communicating their mission, values, and understanding of development. Engaging in open dialogue enables community members and local stakeholders to understand an organization's work accurately rather than viewing it with suspicion. Christian organizations should seek to articulate the development outcomes they envision in ways that are both meaningful to local communities and true to their own mission. The way the organization will practice transparency will depend on the local context, historical relationships, and the community's perception of Christianity. Sensitivity to these factors is essential. The following sections will briefly explore how Christian organizations can navigate issues of trust and transparency when communicating their Christian identity to community members and other stakeholders.

Contextualized Communication

Clear communication means crafting messages in simple, relatable language that aligns with how people understand their own lives and challenges. Misunderstandings and biases abound in areas of faith and religion. To communicate effectively, Christian organizations benefit from first understanding community members' perceptions, knowledge, and experiences of the Christian faith and the church as well as their religious backgrounds and worldviews. To do this well, Christian workers need to become "bilingual" with the ability to translate theological and biblical understandings of development into plain language that resonates with the community. Transparency does not require disclosing everything about why we believe faith in Christ is essential to human flourishing from the outset. Communities may not yet have the categories needed to fully understand or engage with that message. True transparency involves discerning people's capacity to understand and sharing progressively, in ways that invite meaningful engagement over time. However, it is essential that people gain confidence that the organization will not engage in unethical forms of evangelism—such as making assistance conditional on listening to a gospel message or pressuring individuals to change their faith. Through the way fieldworkers engage with them, community members need to recognize that their dignity will be respected, their vulnerability will not be exploited, and financial resources will not be used as a means of coercing conversion. Trust grows when fieldworkers, who serve as the primary bridge between the organization and the community, act with integrity, build genuine relationships, and consistently do what is right. By prioritizing ethical communication, cultural sensitivity, and respectful witness, Christian organizations can build trust, foster authentic partnerships, and contribute meaningfully to holistic development.

Incongruity of Results-Oriented Approaches

Understanding evangelism as relational and embedded within a holistic approach to ministry carries significant implications for how Christian organizations build trust and practice transparency—particularly in how they communicate intent, express faith, and integrate spiritual dimensions. As discussed in chapter 4, many Christian organizations adopt "managing for results" frameworks to guide program planning, implementation, and reporting. These tools often carry assumptions that relationships and expressions of faith, like other program components, can be standardized and measured. However, treating the sharing of faith as a predetermined element within a programming package may reduce the transformational nature of Christian witness to a set of quantifiable outputs. But evangelism, understood as sharing the good news of Christ, is not simply another deliverable. It is deeply relational, personal, and Spirit-led. A rigid, formulaic approach is counterproductive for this kind of ministry. Christian witness, particularly when integrated into holistic development, requires time, prayer, discernment, and the ability to act with humility and love. Harden reminds us that faith-based program theory must allow space for a divine interruption of moments of relational transformation that cannot be fully planned or controlled. Evangelism is both intentional and spontaneous; it involves preparation through training, spiritual formation, and contextual understanding, which can be planned, as well as a posture of openness to the unexpected.

When rooted in respectful relationships and cultural sensitivity, intentional evangelism, inclusion of prayer, Scripture reflection, or theological discussion can be appropriate and powerful. This reflects Harden's concept of integration, in which Christian commitments are not imposed but woven thoughtfully into program life. Evangelism must not be treated as an "add-on" to satisfy institutional faith markers, nor should it be reduced to metrics or externally imposed outcomes. Without discernment, evangelism can distort the holistic nature of ministry and burden fieldworkers with conflicting expectations. It also risks treating local churches as instrumentalized delivery mechanisms rather than as living communities called to bear witness to the kingdom of God.

Christian development should therefore nurture both the intentional and the Spirit-led aspects of evangelism, in what might be called "prepared spontaneity." While tools and systems have their place, they should not constrain the freedom to respond to God's prompting or to signs of people's spiritual hunger. Organizations must cultivate fieldworkers' technical competence as well as their capacity to listen, pray, and walk with people in their journeys. In this way, evangelism becomes part of a broader witness to the person of Christ, who cannot be reduced to a project outcome.

RESPECT FOR PEOPLE IN EVANGELISM

At the foundation of authentic evangelism lies the capacity to see every person as created in the image of God and endowed with gifts and a calling, regardless of poverty, education, or status. Any sense of cultural superiority is not only contrary to the Spirit of Christ but also deeply harmful to the witness of God's kingdom. Respect begins with listening, and it compels us to seek understanding, to observe how people live, to explore the values and worldviews behind their practices, and to appreciate their challenges, priorities, and relationships. This respectful posture opens us to the richness of traditional wisdom, expressed in stories, proverbs, and local histories. When people recognize that we genuinely love and respect them, they are more likely to overlook the cultural blunders fieldworkers and others may make due to ignorance.

Cultural sensitivity must be grounded not in fear or caution but in deep Christ-like love. Visiting Christians should be mindful of behaviors that may be offensive or misunderstood in a local context. For example, though acceptable in many Western settings, public displays of affection are inappropriate in many Asian cultures, especially rural ones. While moderate alcohol consumption is common among Western Christians, most believers in Asia and Africa abstain entirely. Out of respect, Christians visiting from other contexts should refrain from drinking publicly. I recall a persecuted church leader in Laos who once told me, "The best encouragement visiting Christians can give is to avoid behaviors that contradict our local biblical convictions." In holistic ministry, the cultural norms of the host community should serve as the common ground.

Cultural sensitivity is not a substitute for boldness and should never become a pretext for avoiding the gospel conversations. In the early 1990s when I lived in Cambodia, local communities were open and eager to hear the gospel, while expatriates hesitated and assumed their witness might offend. Sensitivity that is driven by fear can become a self-imposed barrier. Sensitivity motivated from love and discernment arises from a respect that opens doors for bold and humble witness to the good news of Jesus Christ.

RELATIONAL APPROACHES

Evangelism, as part of transformational development, is inherently relational. The *Relational Proximity Framework*, developed by Ashcroft et al., offers a helpful lens for understanding authentic relationships and is useful for application in community-based development.[8] It also provides valuable insights into what a relational approach to evangelism might require. The framework highlights five key elements: *Directness* (meaningful face-to-face contact), *Continuity* (relationships built over time), *Multiplexity* (interactions across varied settings), *Parity* (mutual respect and balanced power), and *Commonality* (shared purpose and values). For fieldworkers, flourishing in relationships with God, self, colleagues, and community members is essential not only for program effectiveness but also for authentic Christian witness. Rooted in this relational foundation, fieldworkers are better equipped to share the good news of Christ with both integrity and humility. There are important implications of this

---

8. Ashcroft et al., *Relational Lens*, 148.

understanding of relationships at the grassroots. Here are several elements for empowering fieldworkers to share God's love with people.

1. *Portfolio Assignment for Fieldworkers:* Organizations should carefully consider how many communities or clients for which one fieldworker is responsible. This calculation would account for factors such as cost, whether fieldworkers are volunteers or paid employees, whether they come from local communities or outside, and whether they are technical workers or community facilitators. It becomes excessive when fieldworkers are unable to cultivate relationships or engage directly with communities and must instead rely solely on volunteers to do so. Fieldworkers should have the opportunity to visit and spend meaningful time in each community at least once a week.

2. *Incarnational Living in Communities:* Fieldworkers need to embody and fully engage in the lived experiences of the communities they serve, which involves immersing oneself in the local context, understanding the challenges and joys firsthand, and actively participating in the community's daily life. Incarnational living goes beyond traditional service provision and encourages a deep, personal investment in the community's well-being and development.

3. *Length of Engagement:* Development programs are typically implemented for three to five years depending on funding availability. An engagement of at least ten to fifteen years should be planned to enable continuity of relationships and the development of meaningful relationships that can facilitate transformational changes.

4. *Budget Considerations:* Large program budgets create unhealthy power dynamics between fieldworkers, community elites, and community members. Large budgets may come with expectations for quick results to justify the investment. Resist the temptation to pursue large program budgets and consider instead a low or tight budget that provides sufficient funding for staff, operational costs, and any gaps in funding a minimum of required activities that local communities and partners could not fund. This will allow fieldworkers to focus on building relationships, rather than implementing pre-planned activities and spending budgets. This also reduces the potential power imbalance between fieldworkers and community members.

5. *Reduce Power Differentials Between Fieldworkers and Communities:* Fieldworkers can reduce power differentials by approaching communities with humility, listening more than speaking, and valuing local knowledge and leadership. Building relationships through presence and mutual respect rather than through control or authority helps promote trust and equality. When fieldworkers live simply, share meals, and involve community members in decision-making, they model partnership rather than paternalism. This posture not only affirms the dignity of those they serve but also strengthens the foundation for genuine collaboration.

6. *Fieldworker Recruitment, Training, and Support:* We will treat this topic in greater depth in the next chapter, but it is important to remember that developing and sustaining relationships are actual skills and competencies. Organizations should identify people who have a real heart for people and who are willing to develop relational competencies for their role through orientation and ongoing training. Organizational procedures and requirements should also consider fieldworkers based in remote locations. Relationships are complex and carry with them emotional burdens, and so, fieldworkers need spiritual support.

When relationships are placed at the center of transformational development, a fertile ground for authentic Christian witness emerges naturally. In the 1980s and 1990s, relationships were central to community development efforts. However, with the growing emphasis on measurable results and cost-efficiency, relational approaches have been increasingly questioned and sometimes dismissed as ineffective. For example, in their book *Poor Economics*, economists Abhijit V. Banerjee and Esther Duflo show that home visits can increase immunization rates, but they also claim that the substantial associated costs make such programs challenging to implement on a larger scale.[9] Home visits by development workers may not be economical for scale-up of development interventions, but for TD, home visits are essential.

---

9. Banerjee and Duflo, *Poor Economics*, 62–65.

READINESS AND CAPACITY FOR EVANGELISM

Having discussed the importance of transparency, trust, and relationally focused engagement, we now turn to why fieldworkers must be prepared and equipped to share the gospel as part of their witness. One foundational premise for evangelism in the context of holistic ministry is that regardless of how restrictive a particular context may be, there must remain both a desire and a cultivated capacity for witness at an organizational and staff level. When that desire and capacity are present, field teams should be given the freedom and space to share the good news appropriately as opportunities arise. What are the signs of a genuine capacity for evangelism and how it can be further cultivated? Below are some reflections that are not intended to be a comprehensive checklist, but rather characteristics of organizations cultivating this readiness to bear witness to Christ.

Staff Spiritual Formation and Training

The organization pays adequate attention to recruit staff who are compatible with the organization's mission and values. The organization's hiring practices support the recruitment and retention of Christian staff who are committed to sharing the Gospel, sensitive to the spiritual needs of others, and equipped to offer prayer and spiritual support to those they serve. In addition to personal devotions, retreats, and receiving ongoing pastoral care, fieldworkers are also engaged in regular, systematic biblical/theological reflections in relation to the mission of the organization and their work in communities. Fieldworkers receive training on evangelism within the context of holistic ministry. Staff performance reviews include their intentionality for Christian witness and church relations. Fieldworkers are helped to see Christian witness as an essential aspect of their life and work in communities. Fieldworkers are intentional and have the required capacity to engaging the people in discussions on faith-related issues.

The Role and Place of Fieldworkers

The role and place of fieldworkers in an organization has direct implications for Christian witness. If fieldworker roles are seen as low-status, or simply a stepping-stone to "higher" positions, then their witness of Christ through long-term, relational presence in communities is weakened. By realigning field-based roles, and by recruiting people whose aspirations align with long-term community engagement rather than upward mobility, Christian organizations can better reflect the humility, service, and faithfulness that mark authentic witness to Christ. Celebrating fieldworkers and investing in their spiritual formation, support, and career satisfaction communicates, both internally and externally, that the front lines of ministry are not the margins, but the heart of the mission.

Collaborative Work with Local Churches

Ideally fieldworkers and local churches actively cooperate in a mutually beneficial relationship, and fieldworkers become active members in a local church. Local churches become part of sustainable, ongoing, long-term holistic mission and perceive community development as part of their mission. In communities where there are multiple churches, fieldworkers seek to promote dialogue and cooperation between churches in relation to their witness, mission, and fellowship. Fieldworkers gather churches together to respond to community needs and promote Christian unity. In communities where there are no local churches, fieldworkers and their families gather together to worship and invite others to join if they would be so inclined. Fieldworkers consider partnering with local churches who may be located outside of program areas.

Interfaith Relationships and Dialogue

All religions have closely related dogmatic (what to believe) and ethical (how to act) claims. While the dogmatic claims differ from one religion to another, ethical claims share some basic similarities. Religions also provide normative orientation through values and virtues,[10] which may point to common areas of concern and opportunities for collaboration. Faith leaders hold a unique leadership position in their communities, and they have reach and trust beyond that of non-governmental organizations and governmental entities. Needless to say, an organization should show respect toward people and practices of other faiths and not act in ways that could be perceived as assuming superiority. Honoring leaders of other religions while at the same time communicating a Christian faith

---

10. Schliesser, *Significance of Religion*, 37.

identity authentically may open up opportunities for Christians to share their motivations for development work. Having worked in predominantly Hindu, Muslim, and Buddhist contexts, I have had the privilege of sharing the gospel with faith leaders from these traditions by first earning their trust, treating them with respect, and building relationships through collaboration on issues of shared concern.

Live out the Christian Faith

Faith in Christ and spirituality need to come through in the way that fieldworkers live their lives and relate to each other within their families and their teams and to people in communities, who will see how faith shapes daily life. If it is acceptable, publicly pray before any important community activities. Do not fail to give thanks and glory to God when prayers are answered. Once again, if it is acceptable, offer to pray for people facing specific needs. When people see fieldworkers practice their Christian faith (e.g., asking for forgiveness when they commit mistakes, pausing to give thanks to God before eating a meal or traveling, caring for and spending time with the most vulnerable people in communities), they will ask fieldworkers why they do what they do. Everyday life provides plenty of opportunities to share gospel conversations. For example, Cambodian farmers who depended on rainwater for rice farming once mentioned to me that they were worried because a lack of rain was preventing the transplant of their crops from nurseries to main fields. They mentioned that they had conducted ceremonies in their Buddhist temples, but to no avail. One of my Cambodian Christian staff gently asked them if she could pray to the Creator God who puts water into the clouds! They said "yes," and God provided rainfall the same night. People were surprised by such an immediate answer to her prayer, which provided her an opportunity to share the Bible's creation story and God's miraculous provision for his people.

Use the Word of God

Draw wisdom from Bible stories and Scripture passages that could potentially shed light on specific situations facing communities. The Bible is not just for "spiritual" development, but it can be applied to different aspects of life. For example, the Parable of the Talents encourages responsible use of resources and entrepreneurship, while teachings on family relationships in Ephesians support healthy homes. Principles from Matt 5 and 18 promote peacebuilding and conflict resolution, and Nehemiah's story offers insights on leadership and community mobilization. Passages like Prov 31:8–9 inspire advocacy for justice, and even health-related guidelines in Leviticus can inform modern practices in hygiene and public health. Drawing from Scriptures such as these can help communities find meaningful, contextually relevant guidance for the challenges they face. Rather than preaching a text, fieldworkers can engage people in open discussions by asking questions and exploring how principles from specific Bible passages relate to their daily lives. Encourage conversation by inviting them to share their perspectives and experiences, and allowing the Bible to speak into real-life challenges in a way that is relevant and participatory.

Humble Dependence

Acknowledge organizational and personal vulnerabilities and the limitations of technologies; explain that the organization and its technical programming will not be able to solve all the developmental challenges. Demonstrate trust and dependence on God. Practice spiritual disciplines. Remember to be a Spirit-led community that wears the whole armor of God in this battle against principalities and powers (Eph 6:13–18). Live such lives that people ask questions about the Christian faith. Be prepared to give an answer to everyone who asks you to give the reason for the hope that you have, but do this with gentleness and respect (1 Pet 3:15).

Sensitivity to the Work of the Holy Spirit

God is not limited to program plans, logframes, or key indicators. Always remember that spiritual transformation cannot be programmed or predetermined. Live obedient and faithful lives; love the people that God has called to serve, and remain open for the opportunities that the Holy Spirit brings about. Keep a balance between God's work in the life of a whole community versus individuals. While most program activities might be at group or community level, Christ followers take time for individuals and families in their work. This is one of the reasons that that ratio between fieldworkers and population/number of communities requires careful consideration, which may depend on factors such as the presence of local churches and other believers in communities, population numbers, and nature of program activities, etc.

IMPORTANCE OF THEOLOGICAL REFLECTION

Holistic Christian witness requires providing fieldworkers the space to spend unhurried time with the poor, engage in meaningful conversations, and build authentic relationships. Equally important is creating opportunities for program teams, including fieldworkers, to engage in shared theological reflections. These reflective spaces could explore questions such as:

- What are the spiritual, social, or economic challenges the community faces, and how do they connect to their beliefs?
- How do the community's beliefs about God, suffering, and prosperity shape their responses to poverty and development initiatives?
- In what ways do the people express their understanding of hope, faith, and love in their daily lives?
- What strengths or gifts within the community might God be calling us to recognize and build upon?
- What aspects of our personal behavior and organization's practices might either attract people to or alienate them from Christ?
- How can we honor the community's culture while remaining faithful to the message of the gospel?
- Are there ways we need to change our attitudes or approaches to reflect Christ's character better?
- What specific needs of the community should we bring to God in prayer?
- How can we encourage and involve the local community in praying for their own needs and growth?
- What scriptures resonate with the challenges and hopes of the people we serve?
- What cultural practices align with biblical principles, and how can we affirm them?
- Are there any areas where our own cultural biases might hinder the gospel message?

Such patterns of theological reflections among team members will help fieldworkers remain grounded in the kingdom vision that calls for both personal transformation and community renewal.

MEASURING AND REPORTING ON EVANGELISM AND DISCIPLESHIP AS PART OF HOLISTIC MINISTRY

Monitoring and reporting on the evangelism component of holistic ministry remains a complex and sensitive challenge. The typical quantitative monitoring systems used by Christian development organizations are often inappropriate for several reasons. First, challenges related to definitions make it difficult to establish clear metrics, and the achievement of outputs and outcomes in regard to evangelism and discipleship is often beyond a program's direct control. Additionally, quantitative measurement systems can be counterproductive and lead to perverse incentives that place development workers in difficult or conflicting situations.

If all that we want to do is to count the number of people who have come to put their faith in Christ as part of our monitoring system, it would be hard to discern when they could be counted as Christians. Let me share a story from my own experience. I once worked with a Buddhist, Cambodian agricultural specialist who managed a small, community-based food security program. She was fascinated by Jesus and believed he answered her prayers. She started reading the Bible and grew in her understanding of God's Word. She would often lead her team in prayer and Bible studies. However, whenever I would ask her whether she considered herself a Christian or a Buddhist, she would always answer that she was a Buddhist. She reasoned that her parents had suffered greatly under the Khmer Rouge. They were in their old age, and she did not want to hurt their feelings by making the final step of surrendering her life to Christ and obeying in baptism, even though she knew that was the proper response to the God of the Bible. I am not sure if she ever made a public confession of her faith in Christ or whether it was a fascination that lasted a few years. I knew that she alone would pay any cost of potential distress in her relationship with her parents if she made a decision to follow Christ, and there was no way that I could rush her into a decision. Although counting conversions is widely practiced in Western Evangelical circles, the definition of conversion is much more difficult to discern.

Even if conversion numbers are reported, it would be hard for anyone to check on the accuracy of reported data. There might be a temptation for fieldworkers to exaggerate or falsify the number of conversions in order to impress others and to meet the organization's expectations. Other measures, such as the number of baptisms, the number of people who consistently participate in discovery Bible studies, the emergence of a new local church, or any growth in regular church attendance, would be more objective, allow for trend analysis, and offer insights into what is happening. Qualitative methods, such as the Most Significant Change Story, could be helpful to capture and communicate life transformation stories in context.

EMERGENCE OF A LOCAL CHURCH THROUGH HOLISTIC MINISTRY: A CASE STUDY

In what follows, I will summarize the story of a church that emerged during my work with World Vision in Cambodia in the late 1980s and 1990s.[11] In the early 1990s, Cambodia was then emerging out of its civil war, Pol Pot's genocide, and international isolation. Cambodian churches had just been officially recognized by the government. The church in Cambodia was a miniscule minority at that point of time, but many mature and vibrant Christians refugees were being repatriated from the Thai-Cambodia border. During those early days after the country opened up to the outside world, organizations such as World Vision were required to work in partnership with a government ministry, such as the Ministry of Health, or Education, or Agriculture, etc. World Vision employed program managers and leaders who were always committed Christians, but the rest of the staff—including fieldworkers—were government-appointed staff, all of them non-Christian. The Oudong Health Project was a mother and child health project funded by a public government donor and led by a Christian couple from overseas, but the rest of the staff were not Christians. This Christian couple prayed for the government staff who worked with them to come to know Christ and for a church to emerge in the communities where they were working.

After a few years, government regulations were relaxed, and NGOs were allowed to hire staff from the local population. World Vision then initiated an experimental project staffed by local Cambodian Christians who were recruited from among those people who had recently returned from the Thai-Cambodia border. They were a total contrast to other project

11. Sluka and Budiardjo, "Church Emerging," 47–79.

teams in the way they related to each other, prayed, and studied the Bible together. The Cambodian Christian staff members intentionally modeled the principles of the kingdom of God in how they related to each other. When the Christian couple from the Oudong Health Project took their government-appointed Buddhist Cambodian staff on a peer visit to this experimental project, they were impressed by what they witnessed. One night, the non-Christian staff members woke up their program leaders from sleep and asked them why they had not shared the good news of Jesus Christ with them openly and plainly. The non-Christian staff members told the expatriate Christian staff that "sensitivity" was not an acceptable excuse when Christians had the best news in the world. Upon return to their own project site, they wanted to have regular Bible studies and prayer time. Over the next few months, the government-appointed staff members all accepted Christ, and they started witnessing to their own family members and began seeing transformation. The Christian couple facilitated biblical teaching from Cambodian Christian leaders to strengthen the faith of new believers. They began to see the difference their new-found faith was making in their own lives and those of other community members.

Cambodians practiced Buddhism mixed in with animistic and ancestral worship, and there was quite a bit of spiritual oppression. Several people who were under demonic oppression were delivered. One well-known traditional healer came to know Christ and made a public bonfire of her various instruments. Over a period of six months, there were ripple effects of this conversion of the traditional healer, and around one hundred and fifty people put their faith in Christ. They formed a church with the help of Cambodian Christian leaders. The project staff of the maternal and child health project served their people with higher levels of motivation and compassion. Rates of gambling and alcoholism dropped within the population. As far as I know, the church continues to thrive till today. The following are some lessons learned from the Cambodia case study:

1. **A foundational desire and capacity for witness is essential:** Evangelism need not always be programmatic, but it must be intentional. The Christian couple in Oudong prayed and longed for their colleagues to know Christ, even when their outward expression of witness was restrained. As we saw in the story, the couple's inner readiness and desire—prayerful and hopeful—became the basis from which authentic opportunities for sharing the gospel developed.

2. **Modeling the kingdom through relationships builds witness:** The contrast between the Cambodian Christian staff and government-appointed program staff was a relational witness; it was not technical capacity or theological training. Their love for one another, prayer, mutual respect, and community life modeled the kingdom in tangible ways that deeply moved outsiders.

3. **Openness to the Spirit matters:** What the visiting government-sponsored staff observed as happening among the Christians was not scripted. The government-sponsored staff members' curiosity opened the door for gospel conversations. The initiative came not from the Christians forcing a message but from seekers awakened through lived witness. Sensitivity to the Spirit's timing allowed for a Spirit-led and contextually appropriate encounter.

4. **Cultural sensitivity must not replace boldness:** The Christian couple's reluctance to share openly out of a desire to be sensitive was challenged by the very people they sought to protect. This relational dynamic highlights the reality that sometimes "sensitivity" may be more about the fear of offense. When asked directly, the staff members were eager, not offended, to hear about Christ.

5. **Evangelism is most fruitful when grounded in local community:** The empowerment and mobilization of Cambodian Christian leaders to nurture the faith of new believers ensured cultural relevance and sustainability. The subsequent church that formed was not a Western transplant but organically Cambodian.

6. **Transformation multiplies with spiritual and social change:** The community's transformation was not only a matter of faith but also of personal and social behaviors, namely reduced gambling and alcoholism, increased compassion in service delivery, and stronger family relationships. Deliverance from spiritual oppression and restoration of relationships brought holistic renewal.

7. **Witness is both intentional and incarnational:** This case illustrates that effective evangelism in holistic ministry is both intentional in prayer, modeling, and readiness, and spontaneous in recognizing and responding to Spirit-led opportunities.

WORKING WITH LOCAL CHURCHES, EVANGELISM, AND FIELDWORKERS

In many parts of the world, local churches and believers already exist and bear the primary responsibility for calling people to repentance and faith in Christ. When such churches are present, those local bodies are also called to help believers grow in obedience to Christ's Lordship and to serve their own communities. Churches provide a spiritual home for worship, discipleship, administration of sacraments, and witness, in both word and deed. Depending on their context and gifting, some churches may also initiate holistic relief and development efforts. However, while the church is called to holistic mission, it is not structured as a local NGO, nor should it be expected to meet donor requirements or manage complex, multi-sectoral programs. In such settings, Christian development organizations need to see themselves in the role of equipping and supporting the local church in its holistic witness and ministry. By redefining their primary client as the church and their role as equipping rather than implementing, Christian organizations could help decentralize and democratize development efforts in ways that empower local congregations and embed ministry deeply in the community.

However, the poorest regions of the world often overlap with the most unreached regions, where the church is weak, persecuted, or entirely absent. Many Christian organizations choose to work directly in these areas when there are no existing churches to partner with, both to address material poverty and bear witness to Christ where his name is not yet known. In these regions, the role of the Christian organization is not to replace the church but to plant seeds for its future emergence, by witnessing through word and deed, modeling holistic mission, and preparing the ground for local expressions of the Body of Christ to take root. The absence of the church should not deter holistic witness but should deepen the sense of dependence on the Holy Spirit and the responsibility to serve in ways that honor both spiritual and material dimensions of transformation.

MINISTRY MODELS FOR CHURCH-BASED HOLISTIC MINISTRY

Let us now turn our attention to models of transformational development in communities where local churches are present. These models place local churches right at the center of TD of their own communities. As a result, gospel conversations and development efforts get woven together.

Church and Community Transformation (CCT), developed by Tearfund, the UK-based relief and development organization, embodies the core principles of TD.[12] This approach empowers local churches to catalyze positive changes within their communities, emphasizing the importance of addressing the spiritual, social, economic, and environmental dimensions of development as part of poverty alleviation. CCT assumes that the church has a unique role to play in promoting sustainable development and fostering community participation and resilience. Key principles of CCT include partnership with local stakeholders, participation of community members, and contextualization of the model itself based on local contexts. Local churches act as the local convenors, mobilizers, and catalysts. In the initial stages, local churches are mobilized through a series of workshops that includes biblical reflections on TD and joining with communities and local partners toward a shared biblical vision. Engaging in participatory processes empowers communities to identify their own needs and develop appropriate solutions.

Contextualization ensures that interventions are culturally relevant and sensitive to local realities. Local churches lead a four-phase process: assessment, mobilization, implementation, and evaluation with the end being ongoing transformation of both the church itself and communities. During the assessment phase, stakeholders conduct a thorough analysis of the community's strengths, weaknesses, opportunities, and threats. Mobilization involves building partnerships, raising awareness, and mobilizing resources to support community-led initiatives. Implementation focuses on interventions that address identified priorities and utilize a combination of approaches such as training, capacity building, and advocacy. Evaluation involves ongoing monitoring and evaluation to assess the impact of interventions and to make necessary adjustments. Overall, CCT is a comprehensive approach to development that recognizes the importance of faith, community ownership, and collaboration in creating lasting change. Through the leadership of local churches that mobilize and empower their communities, CCT promotes holistic transformation and seeks to improve the well-being of individuals and communities. Witnessing to the love of Christ is seamlessly integrated into the model.

---

12. Tearfund, "Church and Community Transformation"; Tearfund Learn, "Tools and Guides."

International Care Ministries (ICM), another example of an organization that operates at grassroots level in the Philippines, targets the extreme poor with local churches playing a central role.[13] ICM's approach encompasses education, health, livelihood, and spiritual transformation in a holistic program. They partner with local churches by utilizing a network of church-based volunteers to deliver practical skills training, healthcare services, and education on topics like hygiene and nutrition. The training integrates context-specific and biblical worldviews and values that are essential to overcome poverty and marginalization. By addressing both material and spiritual needs at the household level of vulnerable families, ICM aims to break the cycle of poverty and empower households to lead fulfilling lives. As development work is led by local churches with the support from ICM, gospel conversations become a natural part of how development is understood and practiced.

As organizations establish themselves in communities and build relationships with local churches, emphasize community assets-based development approaches that build on local financial and material resources, human resources including volunteers and networks, and experiences that are accessible to communities.[14] While external organizations may provide technical support or training, exercise caution in infusing any significant amounts of external funding that can bring more harm than help to local churches. What may appear to be a small budget for Christian organizations receiving donor funding might be a huge amount of money that far exceeds a local church's capacity to manage. Injecting large amounts of resources can cause divisions within local churches and with outside communities and subject local churches to suspicion by outsiders. External funding may also create long-term dependency for churches, thereby hindering its witness. Relationships between external organizations and local churches should be empowering in nature without imposing specific management tools or approaches on local churches.

I have highlighted two examples here, though many others exist. God has called the church to be both a sign and an agent of his kingdom, and it is essential that Christian organizations support and equip local churches to serve their own communities—without displacing or usurping their God-given role.

---

13. International Care Ministries, "ICM's Work."
14. Corbett and Fikkert, *When Helping Hurts*, 123–25.

FIELDWORKERS AND LOCAL CHURCHES

In church-based development models, local church leaders and volunteers are fieldworkers, interfacing with community members. Local churches' participation in holistic ministry provides credibility when they share the gospel. Local church members are most likely people from within local communities who have a network of relationships. These models limit the role of Christian organizations, as these organizations may simply provide training and minimal financial support during the initial stages of development work until local churches develop competence and confidence to do it on their own.

However, if programs are initiated and run by Christian organizations with their own staff living in communities as fieldworkers, several implications should be considered:

First and foremost, local churches should be places of worship, fellowship, spiritual growth, and service for fieldworkers. When fieldworkers from Christian organizations participate actively in local churches, it creates opportunities for church members and leaders to become familiar with the organization's mission and work. It also enables the fieldworker to build relationships and explore opportunities for collaboration. In communities with multiple churches, a fieldworker may choose to become a member of one church while intentionally cultivating relationships with others. Active involvement in a local church not only strengthens the fieldworker's Christian identity but also reinforces the integration of faith and ministry within the local context.

Second, local church participation also brings opportunities to nurture partnerships in ministry. Working with church leadership, fieldworkers can identify facilities, land, materials, expertise, experiences, networks, and other assets of local churches that can be used for holistic ministry. For example, a church building, if appropriate, could be used for community meetings, church land used for community gardens, etc. Fieldworkers may help local church leadership start their own community initiatives. For example, fieldworkers serving in a slum within a major city organized a "resource center" that brought together professionals—such as teachers, lawyers, doctors, and others—and connected them with residents in need. Lawyers assisted with housing and tenure issues, doctors and nurses provided medical care, and teachers and graduate students offered catch-up education for children and youth. The resource center created meaningful ministry opportunities for Christians from other parts of the city, while also delivering valuable services to the slum community.

Third, when disasters strike, fieldworkers can help local churches in their role as first responders. Disasters provide an opportunity for local churches to demonstrate the love of God in practical ways. Churches are in an excellent position to offer immediate responses in the face of sudden disasters with their infrastructure and with people who are motived by God's love. Churches have resources and experience in providing emotional support and spiritual counseling to disaster survivors—be it loss of family, friends, or possessions. Disasters can help local churches to transcend barriers of religion, gender, or social status. Depending on the type of disaster and its impact, local churches may be able to meet some of the immediate basic needs or to offer temporary housing for people who might have nowhere else to go. As it is likely that local church members would be affected by disasters, local churches can show solidarity by advocating for assistance from local governments. Christian organizations may come and go, but a local church will remain in a community forever, witness to the love of God, and continue the holistic engagement and that should be the aim.

CALLED TO A FAITHFUL WITNESS

There are no formulas for sharing God's love through holistic ministry. An incarnational ministry characterized by a listening and learning approach provides the starting point. Fieldworkers demonstrate intentionality and capacity for witness to Christ (as appropriate to the context). For nourishment and support in their faith journey, fieldworkers rely on personal, family, and team prayer, reading of Scripture, and other spiritual disciplines. Living in non-Christian communities and engaging in holistic ministry provide incredible opportunities for fieldworkers to witness to their faith through their words and actions. Ordinary, everyday obedience to Christ in small and simple things may raise questions from people for which the good news of Jesus Christ might provide the answer. Fieldworkers' Christian hope can become visible to others through their everyday lives, creating opportunities to share the reason for that hope in ways that are humble and contextually appropriate. Let people see the importance of Christian faith of fieldworkers as it impacts every aspect of their lives. Field staff are wise to resist any urge to rush the process of someone coming to faith in Christ. Pressuring individuals toward conversion can cause deep harm. Instead, space must be made for God to work in his own time and for the Holy Spirit to move freely. They can remain open and attentive to how God may reveal himself through everyday development work.

God does not work according to the organization's logframe or staff's personal plans. Field staff can explain answers to prayers, signs, and wonders that God performs in ways that point people to God and God's love. Evangelism that looks at people's spiritual needs apart from their physical and social contexts is not characteristic of holistic ministry, and neither is development work that does not also communicate God's offer of forgiveness and reconciliation through Jesus Christ. Both physical and spiritual needs should be closely held together in the hearts and minds of fieldworkers.

5

Framing the Fieldworker's Role in Organizational Life

By the time we reach this point in the book, the vision of what is required of a fieldworker in transformational development may seem ambitious—perhaps even overwhelming. As earlier chapters have shown, fieldworkers are the ones who bring the organization's mission to life at the front lines, translating strategies and program plans into holistic practice through both their actions and life. The depiction of fieldworkers as spiritually rooted, relationally mature, contextually wise, and able to navigate complexity with discernment might appear idealistic and beyond what most organizations can realistically expect or sustain. Where do such people come from? How are they formed, equipped, and supported over the long haul? These questions point both to individual capacity and to the organization's systems that shape and sustain fieldworkers. Fieldworkers do not emerge in isolation. They serve within broader teams and organizations whose structures, cultures, and practices deeply influence how frontline ministry is carried out.

This chapter makes two basic assumptions: first, an organization's strategy, structure, and capacity exist to achieve their mission; and second, fieldworkers and their ability to act effectively are vital to that mission's fulfillment. In this chapter, I explore an organization's leadership and development from the perspective of frontline fieldworkers. What kind of internal life must Christian organizations cultivate to support holistic, contextually grounded ministry? What structures and practices help fieldworkers thrive? And what cultural and spiritual conditions enable them to remain faithful, adaptive, and resilient in the face of complex realities?

As was discussed in chapter 2, the book of Acts offers a compelling picture of how Spirit-empowered witness unfolded through local responsiveness, adaptive leadership, and relational wisdom in response to opportunities and challenges that emerged. Rather than rely on detailed strategic plans, the early church expanded through discernment, obedience, and collaboration within changing circumstances. This chapter draws on that same theological imagination and views Christian organizations not as machines to be optimized but as living communities designed to cultivate faithful presence, responsive leadership, and Spirit-guided learning.[1] Fieldworkers are not cogs in a system. They are witnesses, facilitators, and boundary spanners, and they need organizations that nurture their vocation. In the following sections, we explore how Christian organizations can align their leadership, structures, and internal culture so that those on the front lines can live out the kingdom mission with clarity, courage, and joy.

ALIGNING STRUCTURE AND ORGANIZATIONAL CAPACITY WITH FIELD REALITY

An organization's structures are developed in service of the organization's mission. At their best, they do not try to constrain behavior or impose control, but they strive to balance clarity, coherence, and accountability with trust, collaboration, and experimentation.[2] Structures should create opportunities for field-informed learning to influence strategic direction. As discussed in chapter 3, effective strategies often emerge through practice, reflection, and adaptation.[3] Organizations must resist the temptation to over-engineer their structures, systems, policies, and frameworks. These elements should function as scaffolding, not straitjackets; ensure accountability without diminishing discretion; and offer clarity without suppressing contextual creativity.

---

1. Hirsch, *Forgotten Ways*, 18; Roxburgh and Romanuk, *Missional Leader*, 15–16.
2. Schein, *Organizational Culture and Leadership*, 3–4; Block, *Stewardship*, 41–43.
3. Mintzberg, *Rise and Fall of Strategic Planning*, 107–8; Mosse, *Cultivating Development*, 17–18.

Based on my observations over the years, three critical areas frequently divide field staff from the head office: empowerment, communication, and culture. Divisions related to empowerment arise when, despite fieldworkers' invaluable on-the-ground insights, the head office excludes them from key decision-making processes. As a result, a disconnect between organizational strategy and local realities develops. We discussed this issue in chapter 4 in the context of program design, monitoring, and evaluation. Communication gaps arise due to the physical and relational distance separating field locations and the organization's headquarters and branch offices. Field staff geographically separated from an organization's life at headquarters miss both formal channels like all-staff meetings and chapel services, and informal spaces, such as "water cooler" conversations and team celebrations. Creative leaders bridge the communication gap by hosting regular virtual all-staff meetings and town halls, which provide opportunities to share important updates, respond to questions, and pray together as a community.

Cultural gaps can further deepen divisions. Head offices, often based in urban centers, tend to emphasize bureaucratic efficiency and standardized processes, whereas field teams working among vulnerable populations operate in more relational and adaptive ways in order to improve their processes based on new learning.[4] Office-based functions, such as finance, HR, and administration, often operate on separate tracks from field-based programming. These departments emphasize compliance and standardization, whereas fieldworkers prioritize contextual flexibility and responsiveness—two emphases that are not in competition with each other but are incomplete without each other. The result is not just technical misalignment but a clash of cultures—bureaucratic versus relational, procedural versus adaptive.[5] Bridging this divide requires cultivating mutual understanding through regular dialogue, joint problem-solving, and leadership messaging that communicates support services exist to enable mission, not to constrain it, without losing sight of the fact that their effective functioning is essential for fieldworkers to carry out their responsibilities well. Cross-functional teams and collaborative working groups can help bridge operational silos and encourage integration across departments by promoting a shared sense of purpose.

---

4. Edmondson, *Fearless Organization*, 65–66.
5. Fowler, *Striking a Balance*, 115–16.

Aligning organizational structure is a key leadership function, and it must be shaped by insights gained through close proximity to the field. Rigid hierarchical chains of command can obscure insight into frontline realities. Leaders must intentionally flatten structures where possible, visit the field without preset agendas, and listen with humility. Doing so not only builds trust but also signals the deep value they place on the field staff's experience and wisdom. Administrative and support staff should also be given opportunities to experience field realities so that the systems they create remain grounded and relevant. In this way, an organization's structures and capacities become not barriers but bridges that enable fieldworkers to thrive and the mission to be fulfilled more faithfully and effectively.

ALIGNMENT OF ORGANIZATIONAL CULTURE AND LEADERSHIP

While structures shape what is possible, culture shapes what becomes normal. An organization's culture—how power is exercised, how people are treated, what is celebrated, and what is feared—profoundly affects fieldworkers' vocation and effectiveness. As Edgar Schein, an organizational change expert, notes, culture operates not only through explicit policies but through the lived and unspoken behaviors of leaders and teams. A culture that prizes performance over presence, control over collaboration, or certainty over learning can quietly erode the very goals of transformational development by fostering fear and defensiveness rather than faith and trust.[6] For fieldworkers, who serve in relationally complex, unpredictable, and spiritually contested environments, the internal culture of their organization must be one that cultivates trust, grace, humility, and hope. These values cannot be mandated by policy alone; they must be modeled by leadership. As Schein emphasizes, culture is shaped by what leaders consistently do and by what they tolerate.[7] The tone is set not by declarations but by how leaders listen, respond to failure, handle dissent, and model vulnerability. Culture, in other words, is not only what an organization proclaims—it is what its leaders embody.

If Christian organizations reflect the values consistent with transformational development (e.g., participation, humility, mutual

---

6. Schein, *Organizational Culture and Leadership*, 3–4.
7. Schein, *Organizational Culture and Leadership*, 23–24.

respect), then those values must be visible in the everyday practices and relationships within the organization. During my time in Cambodia, one team chose for members to refer to one another using the culturally respectful term "teacher," rather than hierarchical labels like "sir" or "madam." While formal accountabilities remained intact, this small shift nurtured a culture of mutual respect and trust-based collaboration. It was a subtle but powerful way to signal that dignity and partnership mattered more than rank or status. This connection between culture and leadership underscores the centrality of spiritual leadership. In a Christian organization, leadership is not merely about achieving results; it is about remaining faithful to Christ and attentive to God's presence in the work. Ruth Haley Barton et al. speak of cultivating a healthy "spiritual ecology" that invites staff to bring their whole selves to the work and to engage in rhythms of discernment, prayer, lament, and celebration.[8] In this vision, leadership is not simply a role but a posture that is open, surrendered, and listening. Such leadership does not eliminate the need for accountability or performance expectations, but it grounds them in a broader vision of vocation and community. In an organizational culture shaped by love instead of fear, and by grace instead of perfectionism, fieldworkers are more likely to take risks, admit weakness, and grow. A healthy culture builds the inner resilience required to remain hopeful and present in difficult places.

One common source of cultural misalignment arises when administrative systems, originally designed for control and compliance, requires fieldworkers to take extensive time away from their core calling. These systems include financial reporting tools, procurement procedures, Human Resource platforms, monitoring and evaluation requirements, security protocols, and other compliance requirements. While these systems are essential for accountability, stewardship, and organizational health, they sometimes fail to take field realities or the nature of the calling to TD work into consideration. When not adapted to local contexts, they may unintentionally undermine responsiveness and draw fieldworkers away from the relational and contextual focus of their work. In such cases, the burden of compliance can become a barrier rather than a support to the organization's mission. The goal is to realign them, ensuring that administrative processes serve and strengthen field-based ministry, rather than inadvertently constrain it. A good example comes from World Vision India: providing field staff motorcycles and mobile devices and streamlining

---

8. Barton, *Strengthening the Soul*, 125–38.

back-office paperwork enabled them to remain embedded in their communities doing the work only they could complete.[9] These operational changes reflected an organizational culture committed to incarnational presence, trust, and service toward fieldworkers on the front lines.

ALIGNMENT OF FINANCIAL RESOURCES

Sourcing, managing, and sustaining funding is a pressing concern for all NGOs. Many significant practical decisions these organizations face revolve around financial resources. The availability and nature of funding deeply influence strategic choices about scale, staffing, partnerships, and program design. Yet, underlying these decisions are powerful myths in the minds of senior leaders and donors of NGOs: that sustainable development is both quick and inexpensive and that money spent on organizational expenses such as staff salaries, leadership, training, or administration are somehow less important and need to be kept at a minimum. These beliefs are not only misguided but also harmful to the long-term effectiveness of organizations working in complex and vulnerable contexts. The more constraints donors impose, the lower the quality of aid tends to be. In other words, financial resources are not neutral; they carry expectations and limitations that profoundly shape an organization's character and capacity.[10]

Retaining good staff, reaching scale of operations, improving technical soundness, and expanding geographic reach require funds. However, it also introduces constraints that influence organizational behavior, program design, and field-level implementation. In their empirical analysis, Peter Nunnenkamp and Hannes Öhler demonstrate that NGOs operating in competitive funding environments often exhibit greater administrative efficiency by directing a higher proportion of their budgets to programmatic activities.[11] Yet this drive for efficiency can come at a cost when the pressure to demonstrate quantifiable outcomes leads NGOs to prioritize measurable outputs over the deeper, long-term, and relational forms of transformational development. In such environments, fieldworkers often find themselves consumed by reporting demands and compliance requirements, which leaves little space for contextual adaptation or spiritual reflection.

---

9. Sarma, "Experience of World Vision India Fieldworkers," 75–76.
10. Fowler, *Striking a Balance*, 129.
11. Nunnenkamp and Öhler, "Funding, Competition," 81–110.

This tension is aptly explained by the resource dependence theory. It argues that "to understand the behavior of an organization, you must understand the context of the external constraints imposed on it."[12] Organizations are not fully autonomous actors; they are shaped by the resource environment in which they operate. Funders, whether governmental agencies, foundations, or individual supporters, often carry with them implicit or explicit priorities that influence not only which activities get funded but how success is defined and evaluated. As organizations grow and become more reliant on external funding, they sometimes begin to adapt their language, goals, and even mission to align more closely with donor expectations. The pursuit of financial sustainability, while necessary, can gradually give way to mission drift.

This dynamic of mission drift can be particularly visible in resource-rich programs. Fieldworkers in such settings often find their time and energy consumed by the need to meet predefined program targets. Their work, including community engagement, becomes program-driven rather than people-driven. In many communities, this dynamic reorients relationships: instead of being a steady presence among the most vulnerable, fieldworkers prioritize local elites who have the connections and confidence to navigate project structures. Fieldworkers may even come to rely on these elites' support to implement activities efficiently and meet program deadlines.[13] When fieldworkers begin managing substantial funds, they can be cast in the role of patrons and form clientelist relationships, where access to benefits depends more on personal ties than vulnerability or need. Such realities can reinforce rather than transform existing hierarchies.[14] As a result, the very people who most need support may be excluded or sidelined. Not only does the depth of community engagement suffer but also the space for relationship-building, reflection, and authentic Christian witness.

Aligning financial resources with organizational mission requires more than simply balancing a budget. It requires a critical and discerning approach to funding: understanding its sources, recognizing its influence, and ensuring that financial practices remain accountable to the organization's deepest convictions. It means asking not just "Can we fund it?" but also "Should we pursue it?" and "What will this funding require of us?" For field-based Christian organizations committed to holistic development,

12. Pfeffer and Salancik, *External Control*, 1.
13. Mosse, *Cultivating Development*, 110–14.
14. Mosse, *Cultivating Development*, 151; Ferguson, *Anti-Politics Machine*, 67–68.

the challenge is not merely to secure resources but to do so in a way that strengthens, rather than compromises, their distinctive calling.

LEARNING SYSTEMS FOR ADAPTATION AND MUTUAL ACCOUNTABILITY

Effective learning systems that further the goals of transformational development must begin with trust. Learning can best occur in protected spaces for honest dialogue, critical questions, and shared discernment. Learning must not be reduced to a technical task; it must be understood as a relational practice shaped by humility and curiosity. As Professor Chris Argyris argues, organizations that punish vulnerability or suppress uncomfortable truths promote defensive routines that block learning. By contrast, when mistakes are openly analyzed and discussed without fear, deeper organizational insight and adaptability become possible.[15] Amy Edmondson, a leadership and management scholar, also emphasizes the need for psychological safety—a climate where people feel free to speak up, admit errors, and ask questions—as foundational for learning and innovation.[16]

True organizational learning goes hand in hand with accountability. Performance reviews, quarterly reports, and annual evaluations should not be mere compliance exercises but opportunities to ask formative questions: What lessons have we learned? What worked well, and why? Where did we fall short, and what could we do differently? What can we learn from outliers, those who performed exceptionally well or poorly? These kinds of reflective questions invite transparency, deepen collective learning, and prevent superficial reporting. A practical recommendation is for organizations to dedicate an annual day or retreat to learning: reviewing evaluations conducted over the past year and drawing out shared insights. Such rhythms normalize reflection and embed learning into the organizational calendar.

In addition to structured reflection, communities of practice or peer networks of fieldworkers who meet regularly to share, reflect, and learn can play a vital role in shaping a culture of continuous learning.[17] These peer-driven spaces promote practical wisdom, emotional resilience, and mutual

---

15. Argyris, *Knowledge for Action*, 8–9, 101–4.
16. Edmondson, *Fearless Organization*, 15–17, 65–66.
17. Wenger, *Communities of Practice*, 6–7, 126–34.

support. Similarly, project cycles should intentionally build in moments of pause, review, and group reflection and discernment. Ultimately, though, it is the leadership's attitude that determines whether learning will flourish. Leaders who ask real questions, welcome critique, and model vulnerability signal to others that growth, not perfection, is the organizational priority.

Mutual accountability is the natural partner of learning. When framed relationally and spiritually, accountability does not inspire fear. Rather, it celebrates shared responsibility for mission. Fieldworkers thrive when they are trusted, supported, and challenged by supervisors and peers who understand their context and honor their vocation. As Peter Block, a scholar on organizational development, observes, accountability becomes meaningful when rooted in community and not imposed from hierarchy.[18] In this way, learning and accountability reinforce one another and ground the organization in both humility and purpose.

RECRUITMENT OF FIELDWORKERS

Fieldworkers carry both the responsibility for and the promise of transformational development in their daily work. They are the hands, feet, and often the face of the organization among communities—translating vision into presence, programs into relationships, and values into lived witness. For this reason, Christian organizations must approach the recruitment and formation of fieldworkers with deep intentionality. The goal is to discern calling and character and not merely to fill positions based on skills or experience. Fieldworkers who effectively reach toward the goals of TD embody a Christ-centered attitude of service, humility, learning, and spiritual attentiveness.

Recruitment, then, must begin with listening, especially to God and to the needs of the local context. Moving beyond administrative procedures and personnel policies, recruiters can practice a more reflective and prayerful discernment of who God might be calling to serve on the front lines. As Henri Nouwen reminds us:

> The world in which we live—a world of efficiency and control—has no models to offer to those who want to be shepherds in the way Jesus was a shepherd. The leadership about which Jesus speaks is of a radically different kind from the leadership offered by the

---

18. Block, *Stewardship*, 6–7, 41–44.

world... in which the leader is a vulnerable servant who needs the people as much as they need their leader.[19]

Affirm fieldworkers for their spiritual maturity, relational strength, cultural humility, and emotional resilience as well as their technical competencies. Grounding recruitment and formation in this deeper understanding of vocation means fieldworkers will be far more likely to thrive over the long term. They are less likely to burn out, grow cynical, or detach emotionally from the communities they serve. They are more likely to live with integrity, lead with compassion, and sustain faithful presence—even in challenging and uncertain contexts.

Discerning and Selecting the Right Fieldworkers

Recruiting the right fieldworkers requires more than reviewing formal education, technical qualifications, or past experience. While these elements are important, transformational development depends far more on the attitudes, character, relational capacities, and spiritual vitality of the individuals being selected. Fieldworkers must be deeply committed to working among the poor and willing to live incarnationally within the communities they serve by sharing life and not just delivering programs.

A recurring recruitment debate is whether fieldworkers should be drawn from within or from outside the communities they will serve. Alan Fowler, a leading voice on development, civil society, and NGOs, explores the pros and cons of both options. He notes that fieldworkers recruited from outside the community may face a steep learning curve upon entering it and struggle to gain local trust or acceptance. Fieldworkers from outside the community may be primarily loyal to the organization rather than to the people they serve. Conversely, insiders bring valuable local knowledge and deep relational insight, but they may also face credibility issues, especially when they are seen as aligned with an external agency or when inter-group tensions affect how their community membership is perceived. After weighing both options, Fowler cautiously concludes that outsiders may, in some cases, be preferable due to a wider pool of qualified candidates and fewer complications related to social standing or intra-community conflict.[20] Ultimately, the choice between fieldworkers from inside and

19. Nouwen, *Name of Jesus*, 32.
20. Fowler, *Striking a Balance*, 84.

outside the community depends on the kind of transformational change an organization promotes, the context-specific social dynamics, and whether appropriately qualified candidates are available locally. As discussed in chapter 2, the example of Rajanikant and Mabelle Arole, who initiated the Jamkhed health project, illustrates a different logic: they deliberately selected widows and outcast women as fieldworkers within their own communities. These women were chosen because their identities challenged entrenched social norms. For the Aroles' project, the fieldworker's identity was integral to the strategy itself, not just the means of delivering it.

So how do organizations discern and select such fieldworkers? While resumes, interviews, and reference checks can help assess education, experience, and general competencies, they often fail to surface deeper dimensions—such as personal values, adaptability, and emotional intelligence. Reference checks, though helpful, tend to reflect past roles and not future potential.

One effective approach is to design an "immersion experience" as part of the recruitment process. This involves inviting short-listed candidates to participate in selected field activities that reflect the real-life challenges and expectations of the role. These could include staying with a local family for a day or two, facilitating a small group discussion, engaging in community meetings, or shadowing current field staff. These experiences allow candidates to demonstrate their relational engagement abilities, adaptability, and willingness to learn in context. Feedback from the community, existing staff, and the candidates themselves can provide important insights into their fit and potential. Engaging candidates first as interns or volunteers allows the organization to observe their behavior and growth over time and offers candidates space to discern whether this work aligns with their deeper sense of calling. It is important to prioritize candidates who value fieldwork for its intrinsic contribution to holistic ministry and not merely as a stepping-stone to higher organizational positions. Recruiting for transformational development is ultimately a spiritual and relational discernment process—not just a technical one. The right people, in the right roles, in the right spirit, can make all the difference.

FORMATION OF FIELDWORKERS

Recruitment is only the beginning of the formation of fieldworkers. Fieldworkers' long-term fruitfulness depends heavily on how they are formed spiritually, relationally, and practically. Formation, therefore, must be ongoing and intentional. New field staff should be introduced not merely to organizational procedures and policies but to the deeper spiritual vision and relational ethos that bring the organization's work to life. Fieldworkers should be mentored, prayed with, and supported as they navigate the often-complex realities of their role. Ongoing formation should include opportunities for theological reflection, peer learning, rest, and recalibration. Fieldworkers are not simply employees; they are sent ones who are called to bear witness to God's transforming presence in the world. As Steven Garber reminds us, the long-term integrity of vocation rests on weaving belief into practice, identity into responsibility, and calling into the rhythms of daily life.[21] For that to happen, organizations must create environments that nourish both the spiritual and vocational dimensions of the fieldworker's journey.

Where possible, training should be embedded in the field and not limited to classroom settings. Field-based, action-oriented learning allows fieldworkers to develop skills in the same contexts where they will later apply them. Core activities such as planning, budgeting, monitoring, leading community meetings, using participatory tools, working with local leaders, and coordinating with stakeholders lend themselves far more naturally to hands-on learning than to abstract instruction. An effective approach to training involves four steps: (1) provide the essential theory and vision for a task, (2) demonstrate how it is done, (3) support the fieldworker in applying it within a real-world setting, and (4) offer constructive feedback to improve the next time. This "learn-by-doing" cycle not only reinforces skill acquisition but builds confidence and encourages reflective growth. Assigning each new fieldworker a peer or mentor can enhance this process significantly. Shadowing more experienced colleagues allows newer staff members to internalize both the practical and relational dynamics of the role. Mentors serve not as supervisors but as trusted guides—people they can turn to for advice, debriefing, or support during moments of difficulty.

Finally, formation should not be separated from organizational identity. Training in policies, protocols, and standards are best integrated into every aspect of field practice. Organizational values must be embodied in how fieldworkers are equipped, supported, and held accountable across all areas of their role.

---

21. Garber, *Fabric of Faithfulness*, 48–52.

Core Areas for Fieldworker Formation/Training

Based on practical experience, I recommend that the formation and training of fieldworkers in transformational development be organized around the following key modules. These areas aim to integrate faith, community engagement, technical competencies, and reflective learning as a unified whole.

1. *Biblical Foundations for Transformational Development and Holistic Ministry:* This module helps fieldworkers to be grounded in the theological foundations that undergird transformational development. This includes understanding God's concern for the poor, the biblical call to justice, and the integral role of Christian witness in serving vulnerable communities. Training equips fieldworkers to integrate biblical principles into development practice as a lens that informs motivation, behavior, and purpose. Fieldworkers also learn how to engage in theological reflection alongside community members and to draw spiritual insights from real-life experiences and development outcomes.

2. *Community and Local Partner Mobilization and Engagement:* This module emphasizes the importance of community participation, ownership, and local leadership. Fieldworkers learn how to build trusting relationships with community members, leaders, and partner organizations, and how to mobilize them to lead their own change processes. Training includes participatory tools and approaches such as Participatory Learning and Action (PLA), which empowers communities to analyze and act on their own realities, and Appreciative Inquiry, which focuses on identifying and building upon existing strengths, and other community engagement methods. These methodologies promote dignity, dialogue, and collaboration.

3. *Working with the Most Vulnerable and Extremely Poor Households:* Fieldworkers are equipped to identify and support households facing the greatest barriers to well-being. This includes single-parent families, assetless households, street children, persons with disabilities, internally displaced people, refugees, and socially excluded groups such as those considered "untouchable" or from low castes. Drawing on definitions such as World Vision's concept of "most vulnerable persons," fieldworkers learn to recognize indicators

of extreme deprivation, social exclusion, and rights violations, and then to develop strategies to engage communities in inclusive and compassionate responses.

4. *Gender and Social Inclusion:* This module addresses the critical importance of gender equity and the empowerment of women and marginalized groups. Fieldworkers explore how gender intersects with class, ethnicity, age, and other social factors to affect access to resources, voice, and opportunity. Practical strategies are provided for promoting gender-sensitive programming, preventing gender-based violence, and working toward inclusive community development.

5. *Technical Competencies Relevant to Local Contexts:* Depending on program priorities, fieldworkers receive training in relevant technical sectors such as food security, health, education, water and sanitation, livelihoods, or digital tools. Training is context-sensitive and action-oriented so as to equip fieldworkers with the core knowledge and practical skills needed to engage communities effectively and support sector-specific outcomes.

6. *Witness to Christ and Partnership with Local Churches:* Christian fieldworkers are equipped to integrate their faith into their development roles in ways that are respectful, relational, and culturally appropriate. Training helps them embody Christ-like values, such as humility, compassion, and truthfulness, in their daily interactions. In contexts where there is no Christian presence, approaches such as disciple making movements (DMM) can be introduced with sensitivity and wisdom, which will be explained in the next chapter. Fieldworkers also learn how to partner meaningfully with local churches in holistic ministry and to build relationships with people of other faiths around shared concerns and community well-being.

7. *People-Centered Approaches to Planning, Monitoring, and Evaluation:* This module introduces participatory approaches for engaging communities in the planning, monitoring, and evaluation of projects. Participatory approaches involve the active engagement of all stakeholders—traditionally including community members and, more recently, other actors such as local partners, officials, and experts. Fieldworkers also learn to use both qualitative and quantitative tools to assess the relevance, effectiveness, and impact of their work at the same time they foster accountability and continuous improvement.

Emphasis is placed on methods that center local perspectives and learning.

BUILDING A LEARNING CULTURE: THE ACTION-REFLECTION-ACTION CYCLE

An important cross-cutting component of fieldworker formation is cultivating habits of ongoing learning. The action-reflection-action cycle is a powerful approach to integrate day-to-day practice with continual growth. This involves:

- *Action*: Engaging in real development tasks (e.g., facilitating a meeting, implementing a project activity, etc.).
- *Reflection*: Taking time individually or as a team to analyze what happened—what worked, what did not work, and why.
- *Learning*: Drawing key insights from reflections on actions about community dynamics, program effectiveness, or personal performance.
- *Adaptation*: Making adjustments based on those insights and entering the next round of action with improved clarity and responsiveness.

Reflection can take the form of journaling, team debriefs, focus group discussions, or structured after-action reviews. These can be scheduled monthly or after the completion of significant milestones. Over time, this habit improves fieldworker performance and deepens their sense of vocation and discernment.

NUMBER AND NATURE OF FIELDWORKERS

Once fieldworkers have been thoughtfully recruited and formed, organizations need to give careful attention to the scope and the nature of their roles. The number of communities and households assigned to each fieldworker should be proportional to the program activities and budget for which they are responsible. As a general principle, the greater the responsibilities, the narrower the geographic coverage should be. To enable meaningful relationships, fieldworkers should be able to spend a minimum of three to five days per month in each assigned community.

Christian organizations may adopt different staffing models depending on the context and scope of their work. In one common approach, organizations appoint fieldworkers as generalists who have core competencies in transformational development and community engagement. These generalists can be further trained in specific technical sectors that align with the program objectives. An alternative approach is to deploy a mixed team that combines generalist fieldworkers with additional frontline staff, who possess specialized technical expertise in areas such as agriculture, health, or education.

Each approach has advantages and trade-offs. Generalists offer greater integration and coherence across sectors and simplify communication with community stakeholders. However, they may not develop deep expertise in every technical area, even with training. A dual-track approach that combines generalists and sector specialists can enhance the technical quality of programming and distribute workload more effectively, but it may introduce complexity and require intentional coordination to avoid confusion or overlap in community engagement.

A related consideration involves the competency profile expected of fieldworkers. If responsibilities include community engagement and programming as well as administrative functions (e.g., report writing and digital data entry), organizations may need to recruit individuals with higher levels of formal education. These hires increase costs, which can limit the number of fieldworkers that can be recruited. More highly educated fieldworkers may view frontline roles as a short-term step toward managerial or office-based positions, which would mean less longevity and disrupt long-term relationships.

Alternatively, if the emphasis is placed on field-based competencies (relational, contextual, and programmatic), organizations may find it more sustainable to recruit high school graduates or those with modest formal education and invest in on-the-job training. This approach can reduce costs and allow for broader staffing coverage. In many cases, these fieldworkers remain in their roles longer and develop deep roots in the communities they serve as they embody the long-term presence that transformational development requires.

PERFORMANCE MANAGEMENT AND FIELDWORKER SUPPORT

If Christian organizations are to sustain fieldworkers for effective, long-term service, they must ensure that performance management and support systems are shaped by the organization's spiritual and missional commitments. Too often, performance systems prioritize control, standardization, and upward accountability. While such functions are necessary, these systems can unintentionally undermine the deeper goals of vocation, spiritual growth, and relational trust if not held in proper balance.

A mission-shaped performance framework begins by asking fundamentally different questions: How well is the fieldworker living out the organization's values? How is their spiritual life? Are they growing in discernment, relational wisdom, and cultural humility? What kind of support do they need to remain resilient, grounded, and faithful in their context? These questions point to dimensions of formation and fruitfulness that are not easily captured in spreadsheets but are essential for transformational development.

Support systems must likewise be proactive and personal. Regular check-ins, spiritual direction, sabbatical rhythms, mentoring, and access to emotional and psychological support all play a role. Fieldworkers often operate in environments marked by isolation, stress, and moral complexity. Organizations that invest in their holistic well-being demonstrate more than good practice. They affirm the sacredness of their calling and take responsibility for the sustainability of their staff. When performance and support systems reflect the organization's deepest values, they do not merely evaluate, they cultivate. They become channels of grace and promote not just professional competence but deep character formation, vocational clarity, and joy in service.

The process of performance assessment and management expresses the value an organization places on fieldworkers. While compensation and benefits provide some measure of value, thoughtful and mission-aligned performance systems communicate deeper affirmation and development. The use of performance management systems by NGOs is a relatively recent innovation that was adapted from public and corporate models where such systems became widespread by the 1990s.[22] These systems integrate individual accountability with organizational objectives and typically

---

22. Fletcher and Williams, *Appraisal*, 2–4.

encompass the processes of planning, direction, appraisal, development, and recognition. Christian NGOs must reimagine these systems, so they reflect both the theological convictions and the human complexity of fieldwork. As John Swinton argues, in ministry-oriented work, performance must be understood not only in terms of effectiveness, but also through theological reflection and faithful presence.[23] At their best, performance management systems should encourage two-way dialogue, support spiritual discernment, and affirm faithfulness alongside measurable outcomes. The performance management process should celebrate both visible fruit and quiet perseverance and should not only track performance but nourish vocation.

CULTIVATING ORGANIZATIONAL LIFE FOR MISSION

This chapter has argued that the effectiveness of holistic ministry depends both on fieldworkers' passion or capacity as well as the organizational systems, structures, and cultures that can enable or inhibit their work. If transformational development is truly the goal, then Christian organizations must be as intentional about shaping internal life—leadership structures, decision-making practices, cultural norms, and operational systems—as they are about implementing programs in communities. Structures must serve the mission, not overshadow it. Culture must represent the values of God's kingdom—humility, justice, mutual respect, and a posture of ongoing learning—not simply the values of performance and efficiency.

Fieldworkers need more than permission to lead locally; they need trust, strategic space, and relational support to navigate the complexity of people's lives with creativity, discernment, and grace. At every level, we must ask: Do our systems reflect the kind of transformation we seek to facilitate? Do they empower or constrain those closest to the community? Do they help fieldworkers walk humbly with God, listen deeply, and act justly? Reconfiguring organizations according to these guidelines is not just a managerial challenge; it is a theological imperative that requires aligning our internal life with God's mission of restoration and justice and equipping those on the front lines to serve faithfully, fruitfully, and with joy.

While funding, technical expertise, and strong monitoring systems are important, true transformation is ultimately the work of the Holy Spirit, made visible in the day-to-day witness of Christ's love among the

23. Swinton and Mowat, *Practical Theology*, 11–13.

poor. Fieldworkers are at the very heart of this witness. An organization may have eloquent core values, a compelling mission statement, and a well-designed strategy, but without fieldworkers who embody these values with integrity and compassion, the mission remains hollow—like a resounding gong or a clanging cymbal.

As Paul reminds us in 1 Cor 13, love gives meaning to every gift and effort. If fieldworkers do not reflect Christ's heart for those they serve, even the most effective strategies will falter. Wisdom is not merely technical knowledge—it is love in action. Without love that is patient, kind, selfless, and free of envy or pride, even the most visionary plans fall short. Christian mission encompasses both what we accomplish and how we live. Without Christ-like love, all the systems, knowledge, and resources in the world will fail to fulfill the true essence of mission.

Transformational development challenges leaders of Christian organizations to embrace the central significance of Christ-like love in what they do and in how they shape the life of their organizations. Their task is to make wise, Spirit-led choices that enable and equip fieldworkers to embody the values of the kingdom and to serve in ways that are faithful, sustainable, and deeply rooted in love.

6

Catalysts of Kingdom Movements
When the Mission Is Complete

IN THE PREVIOUS CHAPTER, we explored how an organization's structure, systems, and culture can support and sustain fieldworkers engaged in transformational development work on the front lines. In this chapter, we turn our attention beyond the organization itself to consider a deeper question: What does it mean for the mission, not just the institution, to be sustainable? It is rare for international or national NGOs to cease operations because they have fulfilled their mission. More commonly, international NGOs exit a country, or national NGOs conclude a project due to factors such as the cessation of donor funding or rising insecurity. The organizational instinct often leans toward longevity rather than completion and exit. When Jesus said, "The poor you will always have with you," it was not an endorsement of NGO institutional continuity.

By contrast, some mission organizations have modeled a different trajectory. The China Inland Mission (now OMF International or Overseas Missionary Fellowship International), for example, withdrew from China in the early 1950s following the rise of the Communist government, not because the mission failed, but because the indigenous Chinese church had taken root and grown strong despite persecution. In more recent decades, organizations like SIM (formerly Sudan Interior Mission), TEAM (The Evangelical Alliance Mission), and CMA (Christian and Missionary Alliance) have handed over their work to local leaders in several countries where vibrant, mature national churches now lead evangelism and holistic ministry with their own resources. These transitions reflect a core missiological conviction: that the ultimate goal is not perpetual presence, but indigenous leadership and ownership of the mission. As J. H. Bavinck, a missiologist, emphasizes, "The missionary must aim at the disappearance of his own work."[1]

As Christian organizations doing holistic ministry, we must ask ourselves: Are we truly committed to the vision of working ourselves out of a job? Is sustainability defined by expanding our institutional footprint or by cultivating local vision, ownership, and leadership that can sustain transformational mission long after we have stepped back? A kingdom vision invites us to focus on the multiplication of disciples, communities, and movements rooted in Christ, and not on the organization's permanence. In this chapter, we will reflect on how development work can be rooted in a kingdom vision of multiplication, where organizations focus on catalyzing self-replicating movements of transformation and not on perpetuating institutions. We will ask what it takes to make the mission sustainable so that the NGO can fade into the background as local disciples carry forward the work.

Any transformational engagement should work toward the day when the people we work with and minister to become the torchbearers who continue the ministry and extend its impact. Early in my development career, I worked in rural Cambodia on food security programs. After about five years of working in one commune, I had a memorable conversation with local community leaders. As we reflected together on how their village had changed over that time, they spoke of no longer experiencing "hungry seasons," of how their homes now had tiled roofs instead of thatched ones, and of general improvements in well-being. Then we created a "dream map" to envision what their community could look like five years into the future. Toward the end of this lively and hopeful discussion, a few leaders expressed a striking aspiration: they wanted their community to continue developing *and* to help other communities. Someday they wanted their nation to assist other nations. For them, transformation was not only about receiving but also about becoming a source of blessing for others. This moment captured a profound truth rooted in Scripture—that we are blessed in order to be a blessing to others.

---

1. Bavinck, *Science of Missions*, 287.

WHAT DO WE WANT TO SUSTAIN?

Sustainability: A Complex and Contested Idea

We often treat the idea of sustainability as if it were self-evident and universally understood. In reality, it is far from simple. Scholars like Jules N. Pretty argue that sustainability defies precise definition.[2] Others, such as Timothy Luke and Michael Redclift, suggest sustainability can seem like an oxymoron or a political slogan rather than a clear concept.[3] Justin M. Mog portrays sustainability as inherently dynamic, contested, and evolving.[4] Sustainability has become a dominant lens for interpreting nearly every facet of life; it is a comprehensive worldview and aspirational discourse that is marked by its optimism and vision for a better future.[5] Given its increasingly ideological and political usage, it is unlikely that a single, universally accepted definition will ever emerge. Sustainability is best understood as an ongoing, dynamic process rather than as a fixed goal or a destination. As a continual journey of faithful stewardship, sustainability is an aspiration that will never be fully completed on this side of eternity. We should not be paralyzed by the complexity and even confusion that surrounds sustainability. Instead, these concepts invite us into deeper questions: What exactly do we want to sustain? Are we concerned with sustaining organizational structures, funding, program activities and results, or the deeper transformation in people's lives and communities that continues to move forward beyond any single project or organization?

Institutional Sustainability vs. Transformational Sustainability

Alan Fowler provides important guidance for NGOs on sustainability, which he describes as a dynamic integration of ecological, economic, and social dimensions. Fowler emphasizes the importance of local participation, strengthening community organizational capacity, and fostering improvements in material well-being. Fowler also recommends NGOs strengthen horizontal collaboration with other organizations and

---

2. Pretty, "Participatory Learning," 1247–63.

3. Luke, "Neither Sustainable Nor Development," 228–38; Redclift, "Sustainable Development," 212–27.

4. Mog, "Struggling with Sustainability," 2139–60.

5. Caradonna, *Sustainability*, 177–78.

vertical advocacy that influences broader macrostructures.⁶ Fowler's framework is comprehensive, but it also raises an important question: Does emphasizing the sustainability of NGOs themselves risk conflating organizational continuity with sustaining development outcomes? Are the two necessarily complementary or could they sometimes be in tension? This is an especially critical question for Christian organizations whose ultimate loyalty must lie with the advancement of God's kingdom and not the perpetuation of their own institutions.

Sustainability from a Holistic Perspective

Bryant Myers offers a helpful lens by reminding us that communities were sustainable long before NGOs arrived because they relied on their own resilience and survival strategies. More fundamentally, God is the true sustainer. Here is an adaptation of Myers's categorization of sustainability into interrelated dimensions:⁷

- *Spiritual*: Freedom to grow in relationship with God and live according to kingdom values; knowing God through faith in Jesus Christ and their identity as God's children and as members of Christ's body.
- *Psychological*: Growth in self-worth, resilience, and the capacity to influence social structures around them through principled engagement.
- *Social*: Take the lead in driving change across diverse community groups that is supported by capable people and strong institutions and the ability to influence public policies and services.
- *Economic*: Addressing root causes of poverty through asset generation, creation of social safety nets, resource access, and economic resilience.
- *Environmental*: Stewardship and renewal of natural resources without compromising the welfare of future generations.

This rich and holistic vision does not imply that Christian organizations must remain present indefinitely until all these dimensions are achieved. Rather, our calling is to serve as catalysts and to equip local leaders and

---

6. Fowler, *Virtuous Spiral*, 5–16.
7. Myers, *Walking with the Poor*, 192–200.

churches to continue the transformational journey under God's sustaining grace.

Sustaining Movements, Not Institutions

If transformational development is understood as an ongoing, Spirit-led process, and if communities are dynamic and continually encounter new challenges such as epidemics or natural disasters, then sustainability cannot mean locking in a fixed state of achievement or preserving static outcomes. Rather, sustainability should mean facilitating self-sustaining movements of transformation that are rooted primarily in indigenous initiatives, leadership, and resources, as well as strengthening resilience with external support serving only as needed. If this is our vision, it should inform the very design of our engagement from the beginning. Programming should focus not on organizational survival but on nurturing living, local processes of growth, renewal, and kingdom witness.

We should enter a new geographic area with humility and a desire to learn. We seek to discover who is already doing God's work and to identify the people of good will who are serving their communities. Rather than starting with our own plans, we ought to learn from what is already being done. We ask: How can we strengthen and encourage their work? What additional responsibilities could be taken on without overwhelming the existing local capacity? Could we introduce innovations that are contextually appropriate and helpful for the challenges they face? Would carefully chosen complementary resources help strengthen and sustain their efforts or would they lead to dependency?

Walking With and Not Ahead

This vision of sustainability calls for humility, listening, and a commitment to local ownership and leadership. It invites us to see the fieldworker not as an implementer of externally funded programs, but as a facilitator of processes in which the community is in the driver's seat from the very beginning. The following proverb (*mentioned on the left column of the table*), often attributed to ancient Chinese wisdom, beautifully captures the role of a fieldworker in a transformational development process.[8]

---

8. Tzu, *Tao Te Ching*.

Table 6.1—Fieldworker's Role in TD Process

Stage	Fieldworker Role in the TD Journey
1. Go to the people	Enters the community and begins observation and relationship-building; embodies Christ's presence through humility and attentiveness.
2. Live among them	Resides in the community; adapts to their context and culture, becomes a visible sign of incarnational ministry.
3. Learn from them	Actively listens and gains insight into local knowledge and practices; affirms God's presence among them and the wisdom that God has already bestowed on the community.
4. Love them	Builds trust by demonstrating God's love in action.
5. Start with what they know	Encourages use of local resources and knowledge; affirms that God is already at work within their context.
6. Build on what they have	Supports capacity building using community strengths and assets while nurturing spiritual growth and shared vision rooted in faith.
7. When the work is done	Prepares to exit; ensures community ownership and that local communities of faith will sustain witness and transformation.
8. Exit—They will say, "we have done it ourselves"	Steps away, leaving behind a community-led initiative grounded in faith and empowered to be a light to others.

A fieldworker committed to transformational development embodies humility, presence, and relational wisdom that is grounded in a Spirit-led vision of community flourishing. They go to the people not as experts bringing solutions but bearing witness to God's ongoing work. They enter with a posture of listening, learning, and serving. Living within the community, they seek to reflect the incarnational love of Christ, to adapt it to local context, to honor culture, and to build trust. Their work does not begin with externally developed plans but with affirming the gifts, knowledge, and relationships already present. They recognize that God has already bestowed them with gifts. They support communities in identifying and building on their assets as well as strengthening both practical capacities and spiritual growth. Over time, they walk alongside others—equipping, encouraging, and making space for local leadership to emerge. When the fieldworker steps away, the deepest sign of success is not their recognition, but the community's ability to say with confidence and dignity, "We have done it ourselves." This approach reflects a theology of presence and empowerment, where development is locally owned, spiritually rooted, and capable of lasting far beyond the presence of any one organization or individual. Here are some specific roles for fieldworkers with long-term sustainability and Christian witness in view. Each activity points to a vision where transformation is missional and deeply embedded in the life of the community.

- *Mobilizer*: Fieldworkers identify local leaders and resources to bring people and groups together to address the critical limiting factors they face.
- *Connector*: Fieldworkers connect local initiatives with needed external networks, resources, or expertise (when appropriate), without creating dependency.
- *Capacity Builder*: They focus here on strengthening community members' leadership skills, problem-solving abilities, and organizational structures, while preparing them to thrive independently.
- *Cultivator of Local Vision*: They cultivate and encourage a kingdom vision for transformation that empowers local people to see themselves as agents of change in their own communities and beyond.
- *Leadership Coach*: Fieldworkers intentionally work themselves out of central roles; they coach and mentor emerging local leaders to take full ownership eventually.
- *Witness to Christ*: Through their actions and relationships, fieldworkers model the love of Christ in ways that inspire hope, perseverance, and mutual care; they make the Gospel visible even before it is proclaimed.

This vision of transformation requires fieldworkers to initiate and nurture movements that grow beyond them. This invites us to rethink common assumptions about scale and impact. Most organizations and donors involved in international development focus on scale-up of programs and impact as major themes. While we may disagree on how the scaling up needs to happen, we all desire to see the fruits of development replicate and multiply to benefit people without any external organization leading the effort. Jesus compared the kingdom of heaven to a small mustard seed that can grow into a large tree and to how yeast that is mixed into dough causes it to rise. These parables show how the kingdom of God will spread throughout the world through things that are small and unnoticeable. Those who are involved in transformational development work need to bear this principle in mind: it is not about how much we do in terms of program budget and size but how positive changes can be catalyzed and create momentum that can sustain themselves. Our role is not to control the outcomes but to initiate changes that can cause ripple effects. This means that no organization becomes indispensable in this process of transformation. Frontline workers serve as catalysts for multiplying disciples and grassroots communities who live out and spread the kingdom vision and who ensure that transformation is deeply rooted and that discipleship and development are self-multiplying and self-sustaining across geographic areas and generations. Just as the parables of the mustard seed and the yeast illustrate how God's reign expands quietly but powerfully, the replication of transformational impact depends on people who are discipled, empowered, and sent.

FROM PRINCIPLES TO PATHWAYS: EMBEDDING SUSTAINABILITY IN TD

As we reflect on what it means for our work to contribute to sustainable kingdom impact, it becomes important to consider approaches that reflect the core principles of transformational development: acknowledging God's presence and work among people, fostering local ownership including leadership and resources, practicing an incarnational approach to ministry, cultivating authentic relationships, pursuing both internal transformation and material progress, and making and growing as disciples of Jesus along with other principles introduced in the opening chapter. I would like to discuss briefly how Church Planting Movements (CPM) or Disciple Making Movements (DMM) can be integrated with community development here, not as a new theory added as an afterthought, but as a practical expression of the principles this book explores. Christian organizations involved in community development can learn a great deal from DMM in terms of its values, its decentralized structure, and its multiplication potential. More than that, DMM is an approach that can be meaningfully integrated into development practice; it is not just a model to borrow from it. When this happens, we begin to see a more complete model of transformational development—one that holds together both social and spiritual transformation as part of the same kingdom vision. This approach has the potential to catalyze movements that are not dependent on external structures and resources but that grow organically and continue multiplying through local leaders. In this way, DMM points us toward a vision of sustainable mission that outlasts our programs and institutions. This approach honors the image of God in every individual and community and leads to more sustainable, contextually appropriate, and empowering forms of transformation. Such an understanding of development casts fieldworkers not as heroes but as humble facilitators who walk alongside communities and help them uncover and steward what God has already entrusted to them.

DISCIPLE MAKING MOVEMENTS (DMM) AND COMMUNITY DEVELOPMENT

DMM's underlying principles relate to both spiritual formation and development practice. The potential for synergy between these movements and holistic development is significant. This integration offers a pathway to liberate community development from being a domain primarily occupied and shaped by NGOs, academia, donors, and elites. Instead, development can be reclaimed and advanced by local communities, especially local churches themselves. In what follows, we explore this possibility and its implications for practice. DMMs are grounded in the simple, Spirit-led patterns we see in the early church, where the gospel spread through ordinary people gathering in homes, making disciples, and multiplying communities of faith. In recent decades, practitioners began to recover these biblical practices and emphasized local leadership, relational networks, and reproducibility. These movements are not built around programs or external control, but around the vision of self-sustaining, locally rooted transformation. They reflect the heart of the kingdom— where discipleship and witness multiply quietly, organically, and powerfully. DMM is a rapid multiplication of disciples who make other disciples, which results in the formation of new groups or churches that then continue the process of disciple making. DMMs focus on relationship-building, disciple multiplication, and indigenous leadership; DMMs lead to exponential growth of disciples and communities of faith, often in regions with limited access to traditional church structures.[9] In DMM approaches, putting one's

9. Watson and Watson, *Contagious Disciple Making*, 19–21.

faith in Christ is seen as the beginning of the journey, not the end. Individuals may join a house church even before they have come to faith, engaging with others as they share life and explore God's Word together. As trust builds and the Scriptures speak into their lives, many come to faith through this relational and Spirit-led process. Once they put their faith in Christ, the journey continues as they grow in obedience and begin to disciple others—multiplying the movement in their own context. Below is a diagram showing how DMM groups replicate and multiply as each disciple shares the gospel with others.

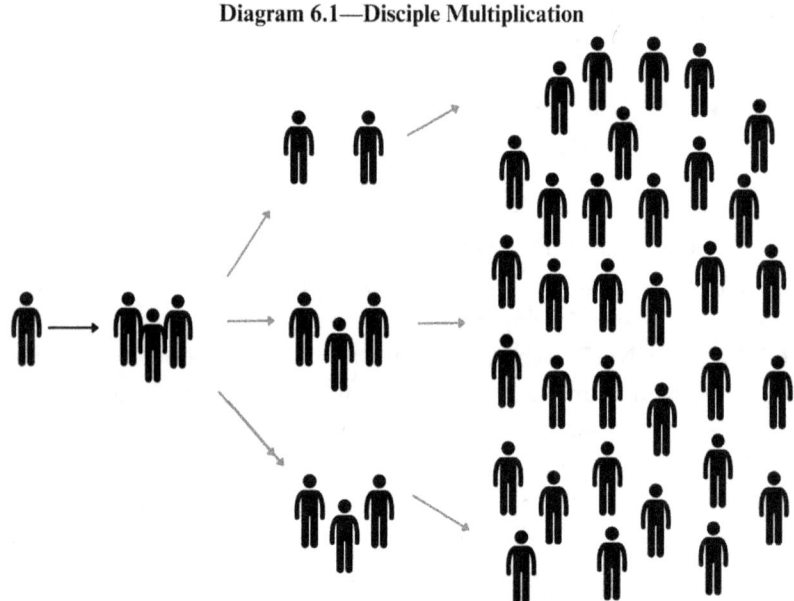

Diagram 6.1—Disciple Multiplication

Common Ground Between DMM and Development

One of the goals of any TD process is to make disciples who seek to obey the Lord Jesus Christ in all aspects of their life, including the making of other disciples. DMM emphasizes local leadership, relies on local resources, and leads to deep and lasting transformation in people's lives. DMM and development share a number of similar characteristics, which creates a symbiotic relationship. Both approaches rely heavily on relationships rather than top-down structures. Built on personal connections, trust, and deep relational investment, the DMM approach entails people sharing their faith within their social circles. Similarly, effective community development depends on trust and relationships in order to mobilize people for collective action. Integration ensures that both spiritual and social transformation happen within the fabric of existing relationships rather than through externally planned and implemented programs. DMM equips local believers to take responsibility for discipling others rather than to depend on outside missionaries or church structures. In similar ways, development is most effective when it empowers communities to solve their own problems rather than relying on external aid. When integrated, both DMM and development reinforce self-sufficiency and ensure that communities grow spiritually and practically in a sustainable way. Both DMM and development efforts focus on equipping and facilitating rather than directing in order to ensure that both spiritual and social transformation emerge from within the community rather than being imposed from outside.

DMM and development work emphasize small groups as the foundation for growth. In DMM, small discipleship groups provide spiritual encouragement, accountability, and space for believers to grow in faith. In community development, small community groups or self-help groups create the structure for mutual support, financial sustainability, and collective problem-solving. By integrating these models, small groups can also serve as platforms for holistic development and help people follow Christ while addressing social, physical, and economic needs together. In many contexts, small groups provide the foundation for savings groups, health education, vocational training, solidarity groups for people experiencing common issues; they offer spaces where trust, accountability, and mutual learning naturally flourish. In some settings, Discovery Bible Studies have evolved into community-led initiatives addressing clean water, literacy, or livelihood challenges, which show how spiritual formation and community development can grow hand-in-hand.

Disciple making movements begin with a few committed individuals who then disciple others, which leads to exponential growth over time. Similarly, community development projects start with small, manageable initiatives led by local people and often see sustainable scaling as communities take ownership. Integrating DMM and community development can ensure that transformation, whether spiritual or social, depends on an organic process of multiplication that is deeply rooted in local engagement rather than relying on large, externally driven efforts. The DMM approach takes root in peoples' language, traditions, and everyday lives. DMM approaches reduce the cultural baggage that comes when cross-cultural missionaries work in traditional communities. Instead, local believers and leadership share the gospel message and disciple other believers. Effective community development also recognizes and builds upon local customs, knowledge, and ways of life rather than replacing them with external solutions. When integrated together, disciple making and development reinforce each other by honoring local culture in both spiritual growth and practical development, which makes change more authentic and sustainable.

Both DMM and community development emphasize working with what is already available rather than creating dependency on outside resources. In DMM, believers use their homes, relationships, and skills to share the gospel and do not rely on large programs or institutions. Community development encourages local people to leverage their existing assets—land, skills, social networks, and traditional knowledge—to address challenges. Integration of DMM with community development ensures that both spiritual and social transformation emerge from within the community and use locally available resources to create lasting impact. Ultimately both DMM and community development recognize that true transformation involves more than just one aspect of life. DMM focuses on the renewal of individuals, families, and communities in every aspect of life. Similarly, a biblical understanding of development goes beyond progress in economic or social aspects of life to address social, emotional, and spiritual well-being. Integrating DMM and community development offers a holistic approach that brings both physical and spiritual renewal.

Multiplying Disciples Who Are also Development Practitioners

For disciple making and holistic ministry to happen in an integrated manner, frontline development workers need to be holistic disciples who mentor others to carry out this integrated ministry. DMM emphasize obedience-based discipleship—an approach to spiritual formation that emphasizes responding to God's Word through concrete action. Rather than focusing solely on getting new knowledge for its own sake or doctrinal understanding, it encourages believers to immediately apply what they learn from Scripture in their daily lives and relationships. In this model, the goal of discipleship is not just to know the teachings of Jesus but to obey them and to pass them on to others in ways that are reproducible and transformational.[10] As frontline workers share the good news and meet with new believers regularly to facilitate obedience-based discipleship, they also help the new disciples to reflect Christ's love in practical ways by addressing poverty, injustice, and brokenness in the community. Disciple making and development are both Spirit-empowered social change processes, which means that the primary resource for such a change process are holistic disciples who love their neighbors and make disciples, not draw from program plans and budgets as their primary strategy. Small amounts of resources from outside may be useful and could be provided, particularly for supporting frontline development workers' travel, training as seed capital for development work.

Making disciples is about equipping people to live out their faith in practical ways. By integrating community development principles into disciple making efforts, we empower disciples to engage actively with and improve their surroundings. As disciples grow in their faith, they can also take ownership of community transformation and lead efforts in areas like savings groups, health and hygiene education, clean water, agriculture, or vocational training while grounded in the reality of the gospel. Teaching new disciples how to love their neighbors in their own contexts and in practical ways—whether teaching useful skills, sharing labor, or facilitating education and childcare—not only meets immediate needs but also breaks the generational cycle of poverty. People experience tangible expressions of God's love and provision and create a fertile environment for the gospel to take root. When disciples see their faith impact every area of life (i.e., spiritual, physical, social, and economic), they can live out their faith in ways that transform both their own lives and their communities. This integration of development and discipleship communicates to everyone that God cares about the whole person and the whole community. The benefits of community development and disciple making can be observed at multiple levels, e.g., changes in individual lives, how they relate to others, use their resources, and live together as families and communities. Small groups of people who are committed and accountable to each other, who also learn, grow, and share lives together, provide important platforms for both community development and disciple making. Let me offer one example from among many on how DMM and holistic development can go together.

---

10. Watson and Watson, *Contagious Disciple Making*, 58.

God's Love Groups in Malawi

God's Love Groups (GLGs) is the name of a local DMM in Malawi. It offers a powerful example of how disciple making and development can be woven together into a seamless, self-replicating model. Each GLG includes eight to ten farming families who gather weekly to study Scripture and to train in Farming God's Way (FGW), a form of conservative agriculture. FGW integrates biblical principles with proven agricultural practices to promote stewardship, sustainability, and productivity. Its management standards emphasize carrying out crop operations on time, to high standards, with minimal waste, and demonstrating the fruit of the Spirit. The FGW technology standards promote conservation techniques like no ploughing, full soil cover with mulching, crop rotation, and precision planting, all of which help restore the land while honoring God.[11] When they follow these principles faithfully, farmers often experience significant year-on-year yield increases and a noticeable restoration of soil health. However, practicing FGW requires a commitment to learning, mutual support, and accountability to uphold its standards; it also requires intensive labor, especially during the initial years of adoption. GLGs plan their farming operations collaboratively and share labor, which is often in short supply in widow-headed households. As community members witness GLG members' practical love, spiritual growth, and improved livelihoods, many choose to join a small group. New participants frequently come to faith and form new groups that multiply the impact.

The movement began under the leadership of Charles, a pastor outside of Blantyre, Malawi. He begins by identifying "persons of peace" in villages, people open to spiritual and practical transformation. These individuals are discipled and trained in FGW and then equipped to lead others. As these new leaders testify to their experiences and teach in homes, more people come to faith. GLGs become hubs not only of spiritual growth but also where people practice acts of love: they care for the sick, tend gardens, and support families during crises. Transformation begins in hearts but flows into the soil, homes, and relationships. GLGs are known for their compassionate response to vulnerable populations. They assist hospitalized members, support orphans, care for the elderly, and help refugees from neighboring countries with housing, healthcare, and farming. Their development approach prioritizes areas of extreme poverty and hunger,

---

11. See Farming God's Way, https://farming-gods-way.org/.

particularly communities with high numbers of widows. Charles believes food security to be foundational to restoring hope of vulnerable people. By restoring soil, increasing crop production, ensuring food security, and proclaiming the gospel, GLGs demonstrate how holistic transformation can take root and bear fruit across communities.

A Village Transformed: The Story of a Chief and His Garden

The following case study illustrates how GLG provided an integrated platform for addressing both spiritual and social transformation while multiplying local frontline disciples. In the heart of Thyolo District, Malawi, where unreliable weather patterns and soil erosion have made farming a fragile livelihood, one village chief found his life turned upside down and then transformed. The village head, whom we will call Mr. N., had inherited his position after the previous leader passed away. Despite his title, he and his family were trapped in a cycle of poverty and hunger. His garden yielded nothing. His children could not go to school. Out of desperation, he had even begun taking bribes to meet household needs, a practice he knew was wrong but felt powerless to avoid.

Then God's Love Groups entered his village. As the village head, Mr. N. was invited to attend their meeting. There, he heard testimonies of lives changed—physically, economically, and spiritually. Moved by what he heard, he gave his life to Christ. Soon after, he joined an FGW training hosted by the group. His commitment was evident, and the GLG came around him in practical love. They helped him clear his garden, dig planting stations, and gather manure, ash, and seeds. When the rains came, they helped him plant. Slowly, the once barren land began to blossom. To his amazement, strong, green crops emerged. His garden became the most productive in the area—fertile, abundant, and well-admired. People began visiting him for farming advice and asked how his life and land had turned around. Mr. N. now testifies: "Everything has changed completely. In my whole community, there is no other garden like mine. It is a testimony not just to better farming, but to what God can do in a person's life." Grateful and transformed, he has committed himself and his family to serving God by expanding GLGs and supporting community development through both discipleship and farming. What began with a Bible study and a few farmers has grown into spiritual and practical renewal.[12]

12. Heaven's Family, internal communication material, December 24, 2024.

Locally Rooted, Spirit-Led: A Movement Beyond Aid

What Charles did not mention in his description is that this organization is not a typical NGO or donor-funded program. Both the leadership and the significant resources come from within the community, specifically from God's Love Groups themselves. An external NGO provided technical training in FGW and assisted with small financial help to help widow-headed households to secure organic manure used in farming. Yet today, Charles leads a growing movement of more than three hundred God's Love Groups that worship together, disciple others, and support subsistence farmers, who significantly improve their crop yields and livelihoods. This numerical increase has happened within a span of three years, and growth continues.

This example illustrates a critical principle: holistic community development is not about imposing external solutions but about helping communities discover and steward their God-given potential. As disciples are made in economically poor and often unreached communities, they are empowered to take ownership of their own development and to address the most critical barriers they face, whether in agriculture, education, or health. External organizations should come alongside local efforts; they can introduce and offer guidance on low-cost technical innovations and provide training and modest seed funding when needed, but always in ways that affirm local leadership, culture, and capacity. This model ensures sustainability because solutions are locally driven and not externally dictated. When communities own the process, the change lasts. When NGOs give handouts to vulnerable people, it will provide only short-term relief and promote unhealthy dependency that is neither sustainable nor empowering. In contrast, when local communities extend help, share resources, and care for their vulnerable members, they create authentic, resilient, and lasting social safety nets. This form of support is rooted in relationships, trust, and shared responsibility; these qualities cannot be manufactured by external systems. Development as defined by NGOs, academics, and elites is formal, programmatic, and constrained by time, space, and budgets. Development as lived and understood by local communities is organic, relational, and ongoing; it is shaped by context, culture, and faith. We must aim for this kind of development: one that flows from within, and is not imposed from without; one that grows through discipleship, dignity, and shared vision.

One of the most powerful witnesses to the gospel is how disciples care for one another in tangible ways. A community that learns to care for its most vulnerable members demonstrates true strength and long-term sustainability. Jesus said, "By this everyone will know that you are my disciples, if you love one another" (John 13:35). Believers show a faith that touches everyday life by integrating disciple making with practical acts of love, such as feeding the hungry, advocating for justice, and supporting widows and orphans. As disciples multiply, so should transformation. Holistic community development becomes a natural fruit of discipleship, rooted in local initiative, empowered by the Spirit, and witnessed by the world.

EMPOWERING FROM WITHIN: RETHINKING DEVELOPMENT FROM THE GROUND UP

Development begins not with money or technical expertise but with a mindset and attitude of caring, sharing, solidarity, and mutual responsibility. People recognize each other's God-given worth and willingly share resources, labor, and burdens. When this mindset of community is present, funding and technology can be catalytic. Without this shared attitude, external inputs may do more harm than good. Too often, development practice contradicts its own values. NGOs may claim to support empowerment and participation, and yet they operate with the assumption that poor communities lack the understanding, knowledge, resources, or agency to improve their own conditions. In doing so, they overlook the deeply embedded patterns of reciprocity and generosity that sustain life at the margins.

A 2005 study across three Southern African countries, titled *The Poor Philanthropist*, found that the poor help each other in systematic, culturally grounded, and morally driven ways. Horizontal philanthropy, the acts of mutual support within communities, follows unwritten but widely respected rules with the majority of exchanges based on reciprocity (65 percent), cooperation (25 percent), and altruism (10 percent). Rather than treating the poor as passive recipients of charity, the study argued that external actors should respect and amplify these indigenous systems of care. Yet this is rarely standard practice. Even in Christian organizations, where faith and transformation are central, integrating authentic witness into externally resourced projects can be challenging. Communities may rightly question whether programs serve their well-being or are simply a vehicle for religious conversion.[13]

What development practitioners need is not just a reform of tools or language but a new paradigm that begins with a community and its vision for life that is rooted in God's reconciling mission. Rather than initiating large-scale projects with external funding and control, Christian organizations can begin by identifying local leaders who are already making a difference: those who love God, serve the poor, and embody kingdom values. These local practitioners are not waiting for instructions, but they do need support, encouragement, and space to lead. This is what the case study from Malawi portrays.

GOD AS THE AGENT OF TRANSFORMATIONAL DEVELOPMENT

In every development program, we find a convergence of stories as Bryant Myers aptly describes. Those of us who come from outside bring our own stories that are shaped by our backgrounds, experiences, and perspectives. The communities we work with also have their stories—rich, complex, and deeply rooted in their culture and context. Ultimately, though, all these stories are subplots within the greater biblical narrative of God's story—the work of God in the world, bringing in the kingdom, renewing all things, and orchestrating everything according to God's purposes. In this divine narrative, God is the main actor. Our role is to align our actions with God's work in us and in the communities we serve. When we embrace this understanding, our primary trust and dependence will not rest on funding, technology, or tools but on God, who is the true author of transformation.[14] To illustrate this, let me share a simple yet profound story from the Bible that encapsulates several principles discussed in this book.

Second Kings 7 tells the story of a widow with two sons who has just lost her husband. Her creditors are threatening to take her sons as slaves to repay a debt her husband left unpaid. Grieving the loss of her husband, she faces an immediate crisis: protecting her children from being taken away and exploited. This story mirrors what we often see in poor communities today when people in power exploit vulnerable women and children because of circumstances beyond their control. It also highlights the harsh

---

13. Wilkinson-Maposa et al., *Poor Philanthropist*, 10–14.
14. Myers, *Walking with the Poor*, 173.

reality that some people seek out opportunities to take advantage of the most vulnerable.

Desperate, the widow approaches Elisha for help. We might think of Elisha as a frontline development worker, but the widow sees him as a servant of God, and his connection with God gives her hope. This perspective raises a critical question for us: How do community members perceive our frontline workers? Do they see them as representatives of wealthy Christian organizations or as servants of the Most High God? The identity of fieldworkers as servants of God is foundational to transformational development. When the widow asks for help, Elisha's first response is significant. He asks, "How can I help you? Tell me, what do you have in your house?" Despite her dire poverty, he begins by affirming that she has something of value—an asset. This conviction—that everyone, no matter how poor or desperate, has something fundamental to contribute to their own solution—is essential for Christian organizations. She responds that she has nothing except a small jar of olive oil, and so Elisha begins precisely with that. This approach reflects an important principle: transformational development should begin with what people have, not with external funding or resources. Similarly, Jesus performed mighty miracles by multiplying or transforming what people already had, rather than creating something entirely new.

Elisha then instructs the widow to borrow empty jars from her neighbors, emphasizing the community's role in her solution. Her neighbors' involvement highlights the importance of collective care and shared responsibility. When communities learn to care for and support their most vulnerable members, especially women and children, they themselves are transformed. This is the goal of transformational development: to enable communities to take ownership of caring for their own and to create sustainable systems of support. Finally, the miracle happens. The small jar of olive oil continues to flow until every borrowed jar is filled. This is God's transformative work—blessing what people bring and making it abundantly sufficient.

Never underestimate the potential of small resources. When they become the foundation of transformational development, the outcomes can far exceed the initial inputs. Elisha concludes by instructing the widow to sell the oil, pay off her debts, and live on what remains. Her immediate crisis is resolved, and her livelihood is secured. Her story beautifully captures the essence of transformational development. When the work is done, people recognize God as the true agent of transformation, and fieldworkers are seen as God's servants.

May this be the testimony of our work as well—that communities point to God as the source of transformation, and we along with frontline workers remain faithful servants in God's story of renewal and redemption.

Bibliography

Ahmad, Mokbul Morshed. "Bearers of Change: The Field Workers of NGOs in Bangladesh." PhD diss., Durham University, 2001.

Argyris, Chris. *Knowledge for Action: A Guide to Overcoming Barriers to Organizational Change.* San Francisco: Jossey-Bass, 1993.

Ashcroft, John, et al. *The Relational Lens: Understanding, Managing and Measuring Stakeholder Relationships.* Cambridge: Cambridge University Press, 2016.

Banerjee, Abhijit V., and Esther Duflo. *Poor Economics: A Radical Rethinking of the Way to Fight Global Poverty.* New York: PublicAffairs, 2011.

Barton, Ruth Haley. *Strengthening the Soul of Your Leadership: Seeking God in the Crucible of Ministry.* Expanded ed. Downers Grove, IL: InterVarsity, 2018.

Bavinck, J. H. *An Introduction to the Science of Missions.* Phillipsburg, NJ: P&R, 1993.

Blair, Harry. "Participation and Accountability at the Periphery: Democratic Local Governance in Six Countries." *World Development* 28 (2000) 21–39.

Block, Peter. *Stewardship: Choosing Service over Self-Interest.* Oakland, CA: Berrett-Koehler, 1993.

Bornstein, Erica. *The Spirit of Development: Protestant NGOs, Morality, and Economics in Zimbabwe.* Stanford, CA: Stanford University Press, 2005.

Bosch, David J. *Transforming Mission: Paradigm Shifts in Theology of Mission.* Twentieth anniversary ed. American Society of Missiology Series 16. Maryknoll, NY: Orbis, 2011.

Byworth, Justin, et al. "Transformational Development Indicators Field Guide." Monrovia, CA: World Vision International, 2003.

Cambridge Dictionary. "Transformation." https://dictionary.cambridge.org/dictionary/english/transformation.

Caradonna, Jeremy L. *Sustainability: A History.* Rev. ed. New York: Oxford University Press, 2022.

Carbonnier, Gilles. "Religion and Development: Reconsidering Secularism as the Norm." *International Development Policy/Revue Internationale de Politique de Développement* 4 (2013) 1–5.

Chambers, Robert. "The Primacy of the Personal." In *Beyond the Magic Bullet: NGO Performance and Accountability in the Post-Cold War World,* edited by Michael Edwards and David Hulme, 241–53. West Hartford, CT: Kumarian, 1996.

———. *Whose Reality Counts? Putting the First Last.* London: Intermediate Technology, 1997.

Bibliography

Christian, Jayakumar. *God of the Empty-Handed: Poverty, Power, and the Kingdom of God.* Monrovia, CA: World Vision International, 1999.

Cooke, Bill, and Uma Kothari, eds. *Participation: The New Tyranny?* 4th ed. London: Zed Books, 2001.

Cookingham, Frank. "Introduction to Transformative Evaluation in Area Development Programs." Internal document, World Vision International, 2009.

Corbett, Steve, and Brian Fikkert. *When Helping Hurts: The Small Group Experience: An Online Video-Based Study on Alleviating Poverty.* Chicago: Moody, 2014.

Courtney, Hugh, et al. "Strategy Under Uncertainty." *Harvard Business Review* 75 (1997) 66–79.

Cowen, M. P., and R. W. Shenton. *Doctrines of Development.* London: Routledge, 1996.

Das, Rupen. *The God That the Poor Seek: Conversion, Context, and the World of the Vulnerable.* Carlisle, Cumbria, UK: Langham Global Library, 2022.

Edmondson, Amy C. *The Fearless Organization: Creating Psychological Safety in the Workplace for Learning, Innovation, and Growth.* Hoboken, NJ: Wiley, 2018.

Eyben, Rosalind. "Hiding Relations: The Irony of 'Effective Aid.'" *European Journal of Development Research* 22 (2010) 382–97.

Eyben, Rosalind, et al., eds. *The Politics of Evidence and Results in International Development: Playing the Game to Change the Rules?* Rugby, Warwickshire, England: Practical Action, 2015.

Fechter, Anne-Meike, and Heather Hindman, eds. *Inside the Everyday Lives of Development Workers: The Challenges and Futures of Aidland.* West Hartford, CT: Kumarian, 2011.

Ferguson, James. *The Anti-Politics Machine: Development, Depoliticization, and Bureaucratic Power in Lesotho.* Minneapolis: University of Minnesota Press, 1994.

Fletcher, Clive, and Richard Williams. *Appraisal: Improving Performance and Developing the Individual.* 5th ed. New York: Routledge, 2016.

Fowler, Alan. *Striking a Balance: A Guide to Enhancing the Effectiveness of Non-Governmental Organisations in International Development.* London: Earthscan, 1997.

———. *The Virtuous Spiral: A Guide to Sustainability for Non-Governmental Organisations in International Development.* London: Earthscan, 2000.

Freire, Paulo. *Pedagogy of the Oppressed.* New York: Herder and Herder, 1970.

Frie, Roger, ed. *Psychological Agency: Theory, Practice, and Culture.* Cambridge, MA: MIT Press, 2008.

Garber, Steven. *The Fabric of Faithfulness: Weaving Together Belief and Behavior.* Downer's Grove, IL: InterVarsity, 2007.

———. *Visions of Vocation: Common Grace for the Common Good.* Downer's Grove, IL: InterVarsity, 2014.

Gaventa, John, and Rosemary McGee. "The Impact of Transparency and Accountability Initiatives." *Development Policy Review* 31 (2013) s1–s28.

Giddens, Anthony. *The Constitution of Society: Outline of the Theory of Structuration.* Berkeley: University of California Press, 1986.

Gorlorwulu, John, and Tim Rahschulte. "Organizational and Leadership Implications for Transformational Development." *Transformation* 27 (2010) 199–208.

Green, Duncan. *How Change Happens.* Oxford: Oxford University Press, 2016.

Grenz, Stanley. *The Social God and the Relational Self: A Trinitarian Theology of the Imago Dei.* Louisville: Westminster John Knox, 2007.

Harden, Mark. "Towards a Faith-Based Program Theory." *Evaluation Review* 30 (2006) 481–504.
Heaton-Shrestha, Celayne. "The Ambiguities of Practising Jat in 1990s Nepal: Elites, Caste and Everyday Life in Development NGOs." *South Asia Journal of South Asian Studies* 27 (2004) 39–63.
Hickey, Samuel, and Giles Mohan, eds. *Participation: From Tyranny to Transformation: Exploring New Approaches to Participation in Development*. London: Zed Books, 2004.
Hirsch, Alan. *The Forgotten Ways: Reactivating Apostolic Movements*. Grand Rapids: Brazos, 2016.
———. *The Forgotten Ways: Reactivating the Missional Church*. Grand Rapids: Brazos 2009.
Hirschman, Albert O. *Development Projects Observed*. Washington, DC: Brookings Institution, 2002.
Honig, Dan. *Navigation by Judgment: Why and When Top-Down Management of Foreign Aid Doesn't Work*. Oxford: Oxford University Press, 2018.
International Care Ministries. "ICM's Work: A Holistic Approach." https://www.caremin.com/our-work/.
Joy, Anish, et al. *Toolkit for Understanding and Challenging Leprosy-Related Stigma for Civil Society Organisations in India*. India: The Leprosy Mission, 2017.
Kilner, John F. *Dignity and Destiny: Humanity in the Image of God*. Grand Rapids: Eerdmans, 2015.
Kumar, Subodh. "Toward Building Evidence of Kingdom Impact." *Christian Relief, Development, and Advocacy* 3 (2022) 24–36.
Luke, Timothy W. "Neither Sustainable Nor Development: Reconsidering Sustainability in Development." *Sustainable Development* 13 (2005) 228–38. https://doi.org/10.1002/sd.284.
Mahoney, Jack. "Evolution, Altruism, and the Image of God." *Theological Studies* 71 (2010) 677–701.
Medcalf, Alexander, and João Nunes. "Visualising Primary Health Care: World Health Organization Representations of Community Health Workers, 1970–89." *Medical History* 62 (2018) 401–24.
Middleton, J. Richard. *The Liberating Image: The Imago Dei in Genesis 1*. Grand Rapids: Baker Academic, 2005.
Mintzberg, Henry. *The Rise and Fall of Strategic Planning: Reconceiving Roles for Planning, Plans and Planners*. New York: Free Press, 1994.
Mintzberg, Henry, et al. *Strategy Safari: A Guided Tour Through The Wilds of Strategic Management*. New York: Free Press, 2005.
Mitchell, Bob. *Faith-Based Development: How Christian Organizations Can Make a Difference*. Maryknoll, NY: Orbis, 2017.
Mog, Justin M. "Struggling with Sustainability—A Comparative Framework for Evaluating Sustainable Development Programs." *World Development* 32 (2004) 2139–60.
Mohanty, Ranjita, and Rajesh Tandon, eds. *Participatory Citizenship: Identity, Exclusion, Inclusion*. New Delhi: Sage, 2006.
Montgomery, John Dickey. *Bureaucrats and People: Grassroots Participation in Third World Development*. The Johns Hopkins Studies in Development. Baltimore: Johns Hopkins University Press, 1988.

Bibliography

Mosse, David. *Cultivating Development: An Ethnography of Aid Policy and Practice.* Anthropology, Culture and Society. London: Pluto, 2005.

Myers, Bryant. "Progressive Pentecostalism, Development, and Christian Development NGOs: A Challenge and an Opportunity." *International Bulletin of Missionary Research* 39 (2015) 115–21.

———. *Walking with the Poor: Principles and Practices of Transformational Development.* Rev. ed. Maryknoll, NY: Orbis, 2011.

Narayan-Parker, Deepa, et al., eds. *Voices of the Poor: Crying out for Change.* New York: Oxford University Press for the World Bank, 2000.

Nouwen, Henri J. M. *In the Name of Jesus: Reflections on Christian Leadership.* New York: Crossroad, 1992.

Nunnenkamp, Peter, and Hannes Öhler. "Funding, Competition and the Efficiency of NGOs: An Empirical Analysis of Non-Charitable Expenditure of US NGOs Engaged in Foreign Aid." *Kyklos* 65 (2012) 81–110.

Oxford English Dictionary. "Development." https://www.oed.com/dictionary/development_n.

———. "Transformation." https://www.oed.com/dictionary/transformation_n.

Pachuau, Lalsangkima. "A Clash of 'Mass Movements'? Christian Missions and the Gandhian Nationalist Movement in India." *Transformation: An International Journal of Holistic Mission Studies* 31 (2014) 157–74.

Parkhurst, Justin. *The Politics of Evidence: From Evidence-Based Policy to the Good Governance of Evidence.* New York: Routledge, 2017.

Perry, Henry B., and Jon Rohde. "The Jamkhed Comprehensive Rural Health Project and the Alma-Ata Vision of Primary Health Care." *American Journal of Public Health* 109 (2019) 699–704.

Pfeffer, Jeffrey, and Gerald R. Salancik. *The External Control of Organizations: A Resource Dependence Perspective.* Stanford Business Classics. Stanford, CA: Stanford University Press, 2003.

Pretty, Jules N. "Participatory Learning for Sustainable Agriculture." *World Development* 23 (1995) 1247–63.

Ramalingam, Ben. *Aid on the Edge of Chaos: Rethinking International Cooperation in a Complex World.* Oxford: Oxford University Press, 2013.

Redclift, Michael. "Sustainable Development (1987–2005): An Oxymoron Comes of Age." 13 (2005) 212–227.

Robert, Dana L. *Christian Mission: How Christianity Became a World Religion.* Blackwell Brief Histories of Religion Series. Chichester, UK: Wiley-Blackwell, 2009.

Roxburgh, Alan J., and Fred Romanuk. *The Missional Leader: Equipping Your Church to Reach a Changing World.* Minneapolis: Fortress, 2020.

Sarma, Jaisankar. "Experience of World Vision India Fieldworkers: Role and Discretion at the Interface of Organisation and Communities." PhD diss., Oxford Centre for Mission Studies, Middlesex University, 2019.

Schein, Edgar H. *Organizational Culture and Leadership.* 5th ed. Hoboken, NJ: John Wiley & Sons, 2016.

Schliesser, Christine. *On the Significance of Religion for the SDGs: An Introduction.* Religion Matters. London: Routledge, 2023.

Sen, Amartya. *Development as Freedom.* New York: Anchor, 2000.

Sider, Ronald, et al. "Holistic Ministry Defined." Christians for Social Action, December 21, 2019. https://christiansforsocialaction.org/resource/holistic-ministry-defined/.

Sluka, Margot, and Tri Budiardjo. "A Church Emerging in Rural Cambodia." In *Serving with the Poor in Asia*, edited by Tetsunao Yamamori, 47–79. Monrovia, CA: World Vision International, 1995.

So, Damon W. K. *Jesus' Revelation of His Father: A Narrative-Conceptual Study of the Trinity with Special Reference to Karl Barth*. Paternoster Theological Monographs. Waynesboro, GA: Paternoster, 2006.

Stroh, David Peter. *Systems Thinking for Social Change: A Practical Guide to Solving Complex Problems, Avoiding Unintended Consequences, and Achieving Lasting Results*. White River Junction, VT: Chelsea Green, 2015. Kindle.

Swinton, John, and Harriet Mowat. *Practical Theology and Qualitative Research*. 2nd ed. London: SCM, 2016.

Taylor, Adam Russell. "Mercy: Where Religion and Development Can Intersect." World Bank Blogs, April 5, 2016. https://blogs.worldbank.org/en/voices/mercy-where-religion-and-development-can-intersect.

Taylor, Laurence, and Peter Jenkins. *Time to Listen: The Human Aspect in Development*. London: Practical Action, 1989.

Tearfund. "Church and Community Transformation." https://www.tearfund.org/about-us/annual-report/church-and-community-transformation.

Tearfund Learn. "Tools and Guides: The Light Wheel Toolkit." https://learn.tearfund.org/en/resources/series/the-light-wheel-toolkit.

Tilakaratna, S. "Animator in Participatory Rural Development: Some Experiences from Sri Lanka." ILO Working Papers 992444033402676, International Labour Organization, 1985.

Tzu, Lao. *Tao Te Ching: A New English Version*. Translated by Stephen Mitchell. Repr., New York: Harper Perennial Modern Classics, 2006.

Wallace, Tina, et al. *The Aid Chain: Coercion and Commitment in Development NGOs*. Bourton on Dunsmore: Practical Action, 2007.

Watson, David, and Paul Watson. *Contagious Disciple Making: Leading Others on a Journey of Discovery*. Nashville: Thomas Nelson, 2014.

Wenger, Etienne. *Communities of Practice: Learning, Meaning, and Identity*. Cambridge: Cambridge University Press, 1999.

Wilkinson-Maposa, Susan, et al. *The Poor Philanthropist: How and Why the Poor Help Each Other*. Cape Town: UCT Graduate School of Business, 2005.

Williams, Paul. "The Competent Boundary Spanner." *Public Administration* 80 (2002) 103–24.

Willmer, Haddon. Review of *Mission as Transformation: A Theology of the Whole Gospel*, by Vinay Samuel and Chris Sugden. *Transformation* 3 (2001) 194–96.

Wright, Christopher J. H. *The Mission of God: Unlocking the Bible's Grand Narrative*. Downers Grove, IL: InterVarsity, 2006.

Yamamori, Tetsunao, and C. Rene Padilla, eds. *The Local Church, Agent of Transformation: An Ecclesiology for Integral Mission*. Barcelona: Ediciones Kairos, 2004.

Index

Note: Page numbers in *italics* indicate figures, **bold** indicate tables in the text, and references following "n" refer to the notes.

abundant life, 5
action-reflection-action cycle, 148
adaptive approaches, 48, 62–63
    biblical perspective, 65–66
    critiques and limitations, 63–64
    fieldworker roles, **49**
    implications for fieldworkers, 64–65
Alma-Ata Declaration (1978), 56, 70
animator, 24–25
Appreciative Inquiry, 146
artifacts of evidence, 84–86

Buddhism, 126
bureaucratic populism, 85

capacity. *See* readiness and capacity for evangelism
cause-and-effect logic in development practice, 50
CCT. *See* Church and Community Transformation
Changed People, 5
Changed Relationships, 5
charismatic model of spiritual activities, 106–7, *107*, 110
China Inland Mission, 153
Christian and Missionary Alliance (CMA), 153–54
Christian identity and mission communication:
    challenge and perception of power imbalance, 111

    myth of neutrality, 112–13
    contextualized communication, 113–14
    communication gaps among field staffs, 136
Christian non-governmental organizations (Christian NGOs), 1, 3, 9, 36. *See also* organizational strategy
    adoption of digital platforms, 76–77
    character of personnel, 12–13
    coexistence of parallel cultures within, 85–86
    communications, 111–13
    demands of strategic management, 98
    about embedded assumptions of tools, 82–83
    environmental predictability in workplace, 95
    and evangelism, 103–4
    external expectations, 79
    Fowler's guidance on sustainability, 155–56
    framing of participation, 85
    Harden's Charismatic model, 110
    internal evaluation, 97–98
    mission and community engagement, 37
    prescriptive approaches, 76
    purpose beyond projects, 11
    rationalistic approaches, 53

Index

Christian non-governmental organizations *(continued)*
  shaping TD processes, 11–12
  and strategic planning, 73–74, 77–78
  sustainable development, 139
  vision and mission in TD, 10–11
Church and Community Transformation (CCT), 129
CHWs. *See* Community Health Workers
Citizen Voice and Action (CVA), 59, 61
CMA. *See* Christian and Missionary Alliance
commonality, 116
communication. *See* Christian identity and mission communication
community development
  biblical understanding, 164
  characteristics, 162–64
  community-based fieldworkers, 20–23
  community-facing responsibilities, 25–26
  facilitation, 24
  fieldworker's work contexts, 28–29
  "ladder of development" strategy, 15
  integration with DMM, 161–62, 164–65
  participation, ownership, and local leadership, 146
Community Health Workers (CHWs), 25
compassion, 105, 112, 126
Compassion International, 20–21n1
continuity, 116
culture. *See* organizational culture
CVA. *See* Citizen Voice and Action

descriptive approaches, 75
development concept, 4. *See also* community development; Transformational Development (TD)
development worker profiles, 38
  Dinesh and Pooja's role, 41–42, 44
  Lamung's pastoral role, 42–44
  Moses's commitment, 38–39, 44
  Ruth's loyalty, 39–40, 44
  Sokchean's commitment, 40–41, 44

directness, 116
disciple making movements (DMM), 147, 160
  characteristics, 162–64
  and community development, 161–62
  disciple multiplication, 161, *162*, 164–65
  GLS in Malawi, 166–69
dogmatic claims of religions, 120

Early Childhood Development Learning Centers (ECD Learning Centers), 67–68
economic sustainability, 156
Education for Critical Consciousness (Freire), 24
emergent approaches. *See* adaptive approaches
empowerment
  field staff divisions related to, 136
  elements for empowering fieldworkers, 54, 117–18
  within organizational system, 169–70
enhancement model of spiritual activities, 106–7, *107*
environmental predictability, 95
environmental sustainability, 156
eternal life, 5
ethical claims of religions, 120
evangelism in holistic ministry, 103–4, 133
  communication of Christian identity and mission, 111–13
  emergence of local church, 125–27
  faith and freedom, 108–11
  ministry models, 128–30
  monitoring and reporting, 124–25
  navigating trust and transparency, 113–15
  readiness and capacity, 119–23
  relational approaches, 116–18
  respect for people in, 115–16
  spiritual activities, integration of, 105–8
  theological reflection, importance of, 123–24

Index

working with local churches and fieldworkers, 128

Farming God's Way (FGW), 166, 168
fieldworker agency, 29–30, 44–45, 102
   accountability in community development, 35–36
   externally initiated interventions, 35–36
   foundational verses, 31–32
   key elements, 30
   key reasons for agency, 32
   limitations in organizational structures, 32–33
   scholarly viewpoints, 33–35

gender
   as agent of TD, 3–4, 170–72
   equity, 69, 147
   literacy intervention, 51
GLGs. *See* God's Love Groups
God
   as agent of TD, 3–4, 170–72
   bearing image of, 31–32
   "God-space," 78
   using God's word, 121–22
   people as co-laborers with, 5–6
   sovereignty, 65
God's Love Groups (GLGs), 166–67
   holistic community development, 168–69
   village transformation, 167
Green Revolution, 50

"Health for All by the Year 2000" strategy, 25
Holy Spirit
   sensitivity to work of, 122–23
   spontaneous spiritual elements and, 105
   transformation development through, 71, 151
horizontal philanthropy, 169
humility, 95, 120, 151, 157
   aligning organizational structure with, 137
   strategic planning and, 78
   TD work in, 6–7, 9

immersion experience in fieldworker recruitment, 144
incongruity of results-oriented approaches, 114–15
inculturation, 22
inner transformation, 4–5
institutional sustainability, 155–56
Integral Mission, 1–2
intentionality, 44–45, 105–6, 132
interfaith relationships, 120–21
International Care Ministries (ICM), 130

Jamkhed Comprehensive Rural Health Project, 56, 70, 144
justice, 8–9, 61–62, 102, 151. *See also* rights-based and justice-oriented approaches

Key Performance Indicators (KPIs), 80, 82

"ladder of development" strategy, 15
Lamay in Peru, TD in, 14–16, 69–71
leadership, 134–35
   action-reflection-action cycle, 148
   assigning households, 148–49
   cultivating organizational life, 151–52
   culture and leadership alignment, 137–39
   financial resource alignment, 139–41
   formation/training of fieldworkers, 144–48
   learning systems for adaptation, 141
   mutual accountability, 141–42
   performance management and fieldworker support, 150–51
   recruitment of fieldworkers, 142–44
   structure and organizational capacity, 135–37
"learn-by-doing" cycle, 145
learning culture, 148. *See also* participatory-learning approaches
local churches
   fieldworker's role in, 120, 128, 131–32
   four-phase process, 129

Index

local churches *(continued)*
    ministry models, 128–29
    organizational capacity, 105
logical framework (logframe), 80, 82, 84

"managing for results" paradigm, 79
    artifacts of evidence, 84–86
    bias toward data, 81–82
    embedded assumptions of tools, 82–83
    fieldworker's reporting progress, 83–84
    strategy to programming cascade, 80–81, *81*
marginalized people inclusion, 55–56
mercy, 8–9, 61, 62, 102, 112
metrics, 74, 76, 92
    emphasis on cost efficiency, 78
    and limits, 79–84
    reporting of field staff, 87, 93
ministry models
    CCT, 128–29
    ICM, 130
modern model of spiritual activities, 106, *107*, 108, 113
monitoring and evaluations (M&E), 80, 102
    evaluation, 129
    ideal scenario of, 99–101, *100*
    people-centered approaches to, 147–48
Most Significant Change Story, 125
multiplexity, 116
mutual accountability, 141–42

Navigation by Judgment (Honig), 94
neutrality, myth of, 112–13
non-governmental organizations. *See* Christian non-governmental organizations (Christian NGOs),

obedience-based discipleship, 164
oppressed, faith of, 109–11
    Christian NGO's recognition, 113
    holistic motives for, 108–9
    missionary work, 111
organizational culture, 47, 151
alignment, 137–39
experience of fieldwork, 27
gaps among field staffs, 136
hyper-regulation of field activities, 28
sensitivity, 116
shift in adaptive development, 64
superiority, 115
organizational learning, 27, 68, 75, 141–42
organizational strategy, 101–2. *See also* Christian non-governmental organizations (Christian NGOs)
    adaptive and responsive strategy, 76
    aligning with TD mission, 98–99
    descriptive approaches, 75
    holding project teams accountable, 95–96
    Honig's criteria, 94–95
    "managing for results" paradigm, 79–84
    measuring TD, 87–92
    mediating strategy and M&E, 99–101, *100*
    Mintzberg's "quantum leap," 77
    prescriptive approaches, 75
    principles for measuring Kingdom impact, 96–98
    quantitative data's role in, 86–87
    Spirit, movement of, 98–99
    strategic planning, 73–74
    strategy to programming cascade, *81*
    transformational approaches, 76
organization-facing responsibilities, 26–27
Oudong Health Project in Cambodia, 125–27
Overseas Missionary Fellowship International (OMF International). *See* China Inland Mission

Parable of the Talents, 121–22
parity, 116
participatory development, 53, 56. *See also* community development
    biblical perspective, 57–58
    educator/animator's role, 24–25

Index

Freirean understanding of community facilitation, 24–25
rise of fieldworkers in, 23–24
Participatory Learning and Action (PLA), 54, 146
participatory-learning approaches, 48, 53
  biblical perspective, 57–58
  bottom-up planning, 55
  challenge of institutional expectations, 55
  critiques of participation, 53–54
  fieldworker roles, **49**, 54
  local knowledge, 56–57
  marginalized people inclusion, 55–56
  shared learning, 56–57
Pedagogy of the Oppressed (Freire), 24
people-centered approaches, 147–48
performance management systems, 92, 150–51
PLA. *See* Participatory Learning and Action
Poor Economics (Banerjee and Duflo), 118
The Poor Philanthropist (Wilkinson-Maposa), 169
Positive Deviance/Hearth approach, 56–57
"power and systems approach," 63
powerlessness, power of, 54
prescriptive approaches, 75, 78
program design, 80
project verifiability, 94–95
psychological sustainability, 156

quantitative monitoring systems, 124
"quantum leap" strategy, 77

RAA. *See* Richarry-Ayllu Association
rationalist-managerial approaches, 48
  biblical perspective, 52
  cause-and-effect logic, 50
  challenge of context, 51
  evidence-based, data-driven interventions, 49–50
  fieldworker roles, **49**
  limitations in social systems and complex change processes, 50–51
  value with caution, 52–53
readiness and capacity for evangelism, 119
  collaborative work with local churches, 120
  humble dependence, 122
  interfaith relationships and dialogue, 120–21
  live out Christian faith, 121
  role and place of fieldworkers, 119–20
  sensitivity to work of Holy Spirit, 122–23
  staff spiritual formation and training, 119
  using word of God, 121–22
relational approach to evangelism, 116–18
relationalism, 85
Relational Proximity Framework, 116
resource dependence theory, 140
"reversal of roles" of fieldworkers, 54
Richarry-Ayllu Association (RAA), 14–15, 70
Richarry-Ayllu ("Wake up, People!") movement, 14–15
rights-based and justice-oriented approaches, 48, 58–59
  avenues for civic participation, 59
  biblical perspective, 61–62
  challenges, 60–61
  criticism, 60–61
  elite capture and unequal benefits, 60
  fieldworker roles, **49**
  tools and methods, 59

secular development theory, 5
secularism, 112
SIM. *See* Sudan Interior Mission
social inclusion, 147
social sustainability, 156
Spirit-led movement/process, 65, 98–99, 157–60, 165, 168
Spirit-led interruption, 102
Spirit-led community, 115, 122
Spirit-led choices, 152

Index

spiritual activities, integration of, 105, 115
   Harden's framework, 105–6
   Harden's typology of integration models, 106–8, *107*
spiritual ecology, 138
spiritual sustainability, 156
spontaneity, 105–6, 108, 115
staff spiritual training, 119
strategic planning, 73–74, 101
   within Christian NGOs, 77–78
   prescriptive approaches, 78
   vs. strategic posture, 78–79
strategy dashboard, 80, 82
substantialism, 85
Sudan Interior Mission (SIM), 153–54
sustainability, 155–61
   DMM and community development, 161–69
   embedding in TD, 160–61
   empowerment from within system, 169–70
   fieldworker's role in TD process, *158*, 158–59
   from holistic perspective, 156–57
   God as agent of TD, 170–72
   institutional *vs.* transformational, 155–56
   self-sustaining movements of transformation, 157
   Spirit-led vision of transformation, 157–60
   rethinking development from ground up, 169–70

TD. *See* Transformational Development
TEAM. *See* The Evangelical Alliance Mission
Tearfund and Christian Aid, 20n1, 129
The Evangelical Alliance Mission (TEAM), 153–54
theological reflection, 119, 123–24, 146, 151
theories of change, 46
   emergent or adaptive approaches, 48
   fieldworkers and, **49**, 66–67
   fieldworkers from implementers to integrators, 69
   integration in practice, 69–71
   organizational conditions for integrative practice, 71–72
   participatory-learning approaches, 48
   rationalist-managerial approaches, 48
   rights-based and justice-oriented approaches, 48
   understanding in development practice, 47
   "weaving a mat" metaphor, 67–69, *68*
traditional model of spiritual activities, 106, *107*, 107–8
Transformational Development Indicators (TDIs), 88
   design principles, 88–89
   lessons for organizations, 90–92
   operationalizing measurement in practice, 89–90
Transformational Development (TD), 1–2, 4–5, 79, 146
   aligning strategy with mission of, 98–99
   aligning with God's mission, 3, 10–11
   church partnerships, 8
   fieldworkers challenges in programs, 36–37, *38*
   God as agent of, 3–4, 170–72
   as holistic work, 7
   human dimensions in, 20
   with humility, 6–7
   incarnational approach and servant posture, 9
   justice and mercy, 8–9
   mutual in effects, 7–8
   people as co-laborers with God in, 5–6
   as process of learning, growing, and changing, 9–10
   reflective questions for practitioners, 13–14
   seeking restoration of relationships, 78
   self-sustaining movements of, 157
   Spirit-led vision of, 157–60

as vision and mission of Christian organizations, 10–13
transformational sustainability, 155–56
transformation concept, 4

United States Agency for International Development (USAID), 76–77

vernacularization, 22
Voices of the Poor study, 60

"weaving a mat" metaphor, 67–69, *68*
well-being, 4–5
    Christian gospel, 104, 109
    external resources, use of, 35
    health and development projects in Peru, 14–16
    participatory development, use of, 53
    science and technology's contribution, 51
work-related expectations, 25
    community-facing responsibilities, 25–26
    organization-facing responsibilities, 26–27
    organization's culture and discourse, 27–28
    work contexts in communities, 28–29
World Vision program, 1, 20–21n1
    challenges of NGO fieldworker's in India, 92–94
    design principles behind TDIs, 88–89
    "most vulnerable persons" concept, 146–47
    organizational culture process in India, 138–39
    Oudong Health Project in Cambodia, 125–27
    partnership with RAA in Peru, 14–16, 70
    TD measurement with, 87–88

www.ingramcontent.com/pod-product-compliance
Lightning Source LLC
Chambersburg PA
CBHW070327230426
43663CB00011B/2244